Words of the Year

Words of the Year

Susie Dent

OXFORD
UNIVERSITY PRESS

OXFORD

UNIVERSITY PRESS

Great Clarendon Street, Oxford OX2 6DP

Oxford University Press is a department of the University of Oxford.
It furthers the University's objective of excellence in research, scholarship,
and education by publishing worldwide in

Oxford New York

Auckland Cape Town Dar es Salaam Hong Kong Karachi
Kuala Lumpur Madrid Melbourne Mexico City Nairobi
New Delhi Shanghai Taipei Toronto

With offices in

Argentina Austria Brazil Chile Czech Republic France Greece
Guatemala Hungary Italy Japan Poland Portugal Singapore
South Korea Switzerland Thailand Turkey Ukraine Vietnam

Oxford is a registered trade mark of Oxford University Press
in the UK and in certain other countries

Published in the United States
by Oxford University Press Inc., New York

British Library Cataloguing in Publication Data

Data available

Library of Congress Cataloging in Publication Data

Data available

Typeset by Graphicraft Limited, Hong Kong
Printed in Great Britain
on acid-free paper by
Clays Ltd., St Ives plc

ISBN 978-0-19-955199-6

1 3 5 7 9 10 8 6 4 2

Contents

Introduction

I remember once hearing a statistic that only 1% of all new words ever make it into a dictionary, and wondering what on earth happened to the rest. In a way, that's what most of my work has been about: finding those words which are on the fringes of dictionary English or which are 'bubbling under', like the old singles in the music charts. It doesn't matter how long they last – if they even rise above the parapet for a short while they are saying something about the time they were born in. They deserve a second glance.

Another memory is of an American college professor telling me a few years back of how he had presented his students with a selection of words coined in five randomly chosen decades taken from the last two hundred years. For each, the challenge he set was to guess both the decade that those words represented and the events that prompted them. The average result, he beamed, was an accuracy of over 80%.

What better endorsement for English's power of description? Many of the new words of a particular time can express often highly complex events and reactions with as much eloquence as any visual representation. They may form a motley crew – put *embuggerance* and *earmarxist* side by side and you get a strange angle on things – but taken collectively their picture becomes a whole lot clearer. Pick any decade from the 20th century and you'll see what I mean: *blues*, *civvy street*, *tailspin*, and *talkies* from the 1900s, *boogie-woogie*, *demob*, *gangland*, and *hem-line* from the 20s, *glasnost*, *lovely jubbly*, *email*, and *Prozac* from the 80s, *bling* and *blog* from the late 90s: all bear the unmistakeable stamp of their era.

The crop of new words from this past year is as articulate as any other. Some, of course, are on the silly side – often the ones we most enjoy (take *Cleggover* and *Boytox*, *nubrellas* and *knorks*). Others, like *run-off* and *cybrid*, are deadly serious. Whichever camp they fall into, they all reflect back to us the topical times. The prominent themes of this past year include ethical living, a global financial and economic insecurity, and the entrenchment of online social networking. All are rapidly generating their own vocabularies.

As these examples already suggest, not all the words in this book are mint-new. It includes older words that have been propelled back into currency, usually because of the catalyst of an event or a social, political, or cultural phenomenon. Each of these familiar, or newly remembered, words has its own history, and some of them have made the most amazing journeys. Who would have guessed that *bouncebackability* would travel from the mouths of a Crystal Palace football manager to the presidential campaign of Hillary Clinton?

Such journeys speak of the dazzling speed at which words fly across the world. Exposure for a new word takes today just a fraction of the time that it did a hundred, even fifty, years ago, thanks to the vast possibilities of the Internet and of blogs, chatrooms, texts, and emails. Far from reducing English to one homogenized, bland lexicon, our language is being opened up beyond all recognition. In fact, as it hurtles ahead, our language is becoming tougher and more expressive than ever, and each year's collection of new words proves it. You may hate *momnesia*, *nomophobia*, *Rickrolling* and *podslurping*: but few of us could deny that, when we heard them for the first time, we weren't just that little bit curious.

Susie Dent, September 2008.

Acknowledgements

If I could thank everyone who had contributed to this book I would, but there are countless nameless individuals who have coined or popularized the words in its collection, making the task an impossible one. They may not even realize their hand in taking English forward, as they surely have.

There is, however, a group of people who have continued to make the collection and research of new words a fun and instructive job: Ben Harris, my editor, and a great campaigner for new English; Helen Liebeck, who did a thorough copy-edit at breakneck speed; Nick Clarke and John Taylor for their creative thinking; Elizabeth Knowles for her unwavering enthusiasm and skill at seeking out both the historical and unexpected angles on many of the words in the collection. I must also thank Catherine Soanes and Angus Stevenson from Oxford's current English dictionary team for the results of their own language monitoring, and Graeme Diamond and his team from the *Oxford English Dictionary* for theirs. Their unending watch of English's developments is at the heart of the book.

Notes on trademarks and proprietary status

The Words of the Year

adventure running
arguido/arguida
bacn
beaut
beni
Boytox
churnalism
Cleggover
cripes
cybrid
data exhaust
drawdown
earmarxist
ecotown
embuggerance
entente amicale
ethicurean
exergame
exoplanet
facebook
femtocell
flame attendant
freeconomics
freemale
free range kid
frogamander
glamping
God's access
googleability
Googlegänger

800lb gorilla
HIP
homedebtor
IPOD
ish
jingle mail
junk sleep
kinnear
knork
latte liberal
lifestream
limbo skating
locavore
McQualification
manscaping
misspeak
momnesia
moofer
mosquito
mullet strategy
nanofood
Nerdic
NINJA loan
nomophobia
non-dom
nonebrity
nubrella
olderpreneur
peaknik
PICNIC

podslurping
polyclinics
pond swooping
Poolates
popcorn lung
potwalloping
purrcast
Rickrolling
run-off
schwag
scuppie
shoefiti
shopdropping
showa

sleevefacing
slow medicine
speed mentoring
speedriding
T5
toff
treggings
umbilicoplasty
undo-plasty
vuvuzela
wavefarm
webcom
WiMax
YAOI

adventure running

the sport of running over a variety of surfaces, such as dirt tracks and mountains.

The idea of **adventure running** is to take nature on and to defy it. The challenges faced by adventure runners might include steep mountain passes, river crossings, snow, and high altitudes.

Although well established, adventure running has come into its own as the search of extreme sports gathers ever more momentum. Tough expedition races for the elite are making adventure running one of the UK's fastest-growing sports. Recently staged races take on some of the world's most challenging terrains, from the Andes to Alaska and the Namibian Skeleton Coast (billed as 'a 120 km race over 24 hours through the most hostile desert coastline on the planet').

Ultra-running**, and even **extreme ultra-running**, are further options for those runners looking for extra edge. Used to define any race over the distance of a marathon, an 'ultra-run' might also involve arduous terrain, elevation changes, or navigational challenges.

Meanwhile, **urban adventure racing**, or **rat racing**, is the city offshoot of adventure running. Dangling from office-block roofs or abseiling from a crane may be a leap away from the norm but, as one participant put it, 'it beats your average open-topped bus tour'.

arguido/arguida

(from the Portuguese) a named suspect in a criminal investigation.

An **arguido** or **arguida** (the former male, the latter female) is a Portuguese term usually translated as 'named suspect' or 'formal suspect'. It designates a status in the Portuguese legal system which is distinct from that of a general suspect. The individual concerned is treated as more than a witness but is not formally charged. The designation provides certain legal protection that is not extended to a witness, including the right to remain silent during questioning and the right to legal representation.

The term 'arguido' has become naturalized in English as a result of the investigation by Portuguese police into the disappearance of 3-year-old Madeleine McCann while on holiday in the Algarve, during which the status was invoked upon three people, including her parents Kate and Gerry McCann. (It was later retracted.)

The speed with which the term entered English vocabulary was a reflection both of the enormous public interest in the McCann case and of the media's ready integration of the term into its press reports. It has now gained sufficiently common currency that an explanation of the term is largely unnecessary. This naturalization of a term which was hitherto largely unfamiliar shows just how readily English absorbs terms from other cultures when they are needed, and when no translation can easily convey their meaning.

The majority of words used in English today are of foreign origin, historically from Latin and Greek and in more recent centuries from almost all the languages of Europe. Approximately 5% of all new words in the 20th century came from abroad, and many were from far and exotic countries of the world. In total, over 120 languages are on record as sources of modern-day English vocabulary.

The majority of so-called 'loan words' come about as a result of cultural influence, and lifestyle terms are particularly likely to be picked up. Food, sports, fashion, fitness regimes, and health remedies and therapies are all areas where English is currently hoovering up foreign terms most rapidly. Recent food imports, for example, include the **açai** (a fruit from the Amazon region), the **kaiseki** (a traditional multi-course Japanese meal), and the **ristretto** (a very short shot of espresso coffee).

When a foreign word comes out of a prominent event its exposure is guaranteed. As a result, it stands an excellent chance of becoming absorbed into our language and 'naturalized'. 'Arguido/arguida' certainly fits into this category. Another example, also from tragic circumstances, is likely to evoke today for millions of English speakers the very specific and shocking effects of the events in Asia in the closing days of 2004: **tsunami**.

'Tsunami', before the disastrous earthquake, was a term largely confined to the vocabulary of seismologists and geographers. It is Japanese for 'harbour' (*tsu*) 'wave' (*nami*), but its literal definition was quickly extended to mean anything colossal or powerful.

The language arising from a significant event can become a distillation of the event itself. 'Arguido/arguida', like 'tsunami', is likely to carry with it a whole host of tragic associations for some time to come.

bacn

(pronounced as 'bacon') impersonal email and text messages, such as automatic notifications and newsletters, that have been subscribed to but which are left unopened by the recipient for a long time.

Bacn has been described as 'email that you want, but not right now'. As opposed to **spam**, which is unsolicited, bacn consists of low-priority automated messages which are expected but which are usually left for later. Such messages might include new friend notifications on social networking sites such as *Facebook*, newsletters from clubs and associations, Google alerts on the subjects we have chosen to hear about, or fashion bulletins from our favourite clothes shop. We know we ought to read it, and that we may even enjoy it when we do, but not right now.

Pronounced like 'bacon', and so with a deliberate connection with spam, 'bacn' is used as an uncountable noun. It was coined in August 2007, at PodCamp Pittsburgh. (**PodCamp** is a term used in the online community for an informal conference for networking, attended by those who participate in such online activities as blogging, podcasting, facebooking, and other kinds of social networking.)

The potential of what has been called 'middle-class email' (neither personal nor unwanted) to clutter our inboxes is huge. As a result, solutions for managing bacn may well become big business, and websites dedicated to bacn management are multiplying. The term's linguistic future also looks promising, given its proliferation on the Web (there is an official 'bacn' site) and its emerging derivatives. We are already hearing about **FakinBacn**: bacn which is really spam in disguise.

The word 'bacn' was chosen because it extends the rather curious meat metaphor which began with the expression 'spam'. A blend of 'spiced' and 'ham', spam originally referred to a brand of tinned meat which is particularly associated with World War II rations, at a time when meat was in short supply. Its use in computing, to denote unwanted email, comes from a *Monty Python* sketch in which two customers are ordering breakfast which includes the processed meat spam in almost every dish. The junk mail which floods our inbox reflects the idea of the repetitive and undesirable occurrence of spam in the sketch.

Several other computing terms were born out of the spam idea. **Ham** refers to legitimate email messages which are real (as the meat is) compared with the 'fake' spam. On the same theme, **meatloaf** is unsolicited email from one individual which is then forwarded to a large number of people. This might include family round-robins, jokes, or silly anecdotes: for meatloaf is, of course, homemade.

As for bacn on the real vs fake meat scale, it clearly falls somewhere between spam and ham.

beaut

an idiot.

Beaut is very definitely a local Liverpool term and, like so much of its dialect, one that is shot through with a splash of irony. An abbreviation of 'beauty' and/or 'beautiful', it is reminiscent of the far older term 'natural', which similarly used to denote a fool or the very opposite of what it appears to suggest.

Unsurprisingly perhaps, the other primary users of 'beaut' as a noun are Australians, where the word ranks with **cobber** as one of the nation's linguistic badges. Although here it is used in its non-ironic sense of something positive, the sense of 'a self-righteous know-it-all' (to quote one Australian blog) is definitely out there. Indeed, there may yet be a Liverpudlian link via Ireland – Liverpool has a large Irish community and early Australia had a heavy concentration of Irish immigrants, voluntary or otherwise.

For those Scousers for whom 'beaut' is simply the latest in a long heritage of locally-inspired slang, it pays to remember the past. The *Liverpool Echo* recently put it thus:

'How many times have you called someone a "belter", a "biff", a "blurt", a "beaut" or the truly cutting "ya, no-mark"? But nothing comes close to the genius that are proper old school Scouse insults. Most are hardly used today, but the likes of "balloon-head", "pleb", the legendary "divvie" and the now politically incorrect but once hugely popular "meff" still stand alone as Scouse slang silverware.'

beni

a lipstick from Japan recently launched in the British market.

'Solid, green and iridescent, it bears little resemblance to a standard lipstick.
But for hundreds of years, Japan's geisha would never leave home without
dipping a wet brush into a natural compound called **beni** to create a rich
paint for their trademark red lips.'

So wrote Danielle Demetriou for *The Daily Telegraph* in the spring
of 2008, days before one of the geisha girls' hitherto biggest
secrets was launched onto the worldwide cosmetics market. Beni, a
paste formed from crushed and steamed safflower petals, produces
an ultra-bright shade of vermilion on contact with water. The
resulting colour, when applied to lips, can apparently withstand the
toughest of daily activities such as tea-drinking, eating, and kissing.

From the early 17th century on, generations of geisha and other
Japanese women used beni to paint their lips, cheeks, eyes, and
nails. When even Japanese women fell for the handier lipsticks of the
West, however, beni all but disappeared. Until now.

For those excited by the chance to emulate the stars of recent
film successes such as *Memoirs of a Geisha*, however, there is
a sticking point: beni is one of the most expensive lipsticks in the
world, presented as it is in ornate, lacquered cases designed by top
Japanese artists. Nonetheless, the price of £335 for one lipstick and
up to £1,500 for a pot may put off even the most tempted of women:
that means an evening's use could cost around £50.

Boytox

Botox cosmetic treatment for men.

According to statistics published in March 2008, a fifth of all Britons who undergo Botox treatment as an anti-ageing measure are men. Not only that, but the figure of 20,000 reflects a 50% increase over the previous twelve months.

Such a growing phenomenon, which means big business for the cosmetics industry, almost demanded a new name. **Boytox** joins other terms in the new male grooming lexicon including, from the early noughties, the **back, sack, and crack**: a waxing procedure by which a man's body hair is removed from his back, genitals, and between his buttocks, alternatively known as the **boyzilian**.

Terms such as these sit alongside the new various types of modern male. **Metrosexuals**, who spend a lot of time on their appearance and whose ranks are said to include David Beckham, are the most likely seekers of Boytox. It is, however, unlikely to appeal to **machosexuals**: 'blokeish' men who spend as little time and money on their appearance as possible and who yearn for adventure with the same passion that metrosexuals do grooming products. **Retrosexuals**, of course, care for neither.

See also MANSCAPING.

churnalism

a category of journalism in which stories are repeated second-hand without primary research.

It is Nick Davies in his book *Flat Earth* whom we can thank for the term **churnalism**, coined as a result of the falling standards he perceives in today's journalism. Davies, a reporter for *The Guardian*, led a survey of some 2,000 news stories conducted by Cardiff University's journalism department. The result: 80% of home news stories in the main 'quality' newspapers are either partially or entirely made up of recycled material.

Nick Davies concluded: 'Where once journalists were active gatherers of news, now they have generally become mere passive processors of unchecked, second-hand material, much of it contrived by PR to serve some political or commercial interest. Not journalists, but **churnalists**.' In other words, the newspaper industry is now one which is highly vulnerable to manipulation and thus to the perpetuation of distortion and propaganda.

Strong stuff, but Cardiff's finding that the average Fleet Street journalist now has to fill three times as much space as they did back in 1985 – thanks to swingeing staffing cuts – is surely food for thought. If Davies and his team wanted to bring this dramatically home, then creating a new term was a highly effective way of doing it.

Cleggover

the nickname given to the new Liberal Democrat leader
Nick Clegg following an interview in *GQ* magazine, in
which he revealed that he had slept with up to 30 women.

*T*he Sun, under the headline 'Lib Dem Nick's **Cleggovers**',
recalled the admission by former Tory leader William Hague to
the same magazine that 'he sank as many as 14 pints of beer a day
while delivering booze to pubs in a student holiday job'.

Kevin Maguire, meanwhile, writing in the *New Statesman*, wrote
in his wry 'Westminster gossip' column: 'That Lib Dem sexpot
Nick Cleggover is on the prowl. The whisper is that the Sheffield stud
is seeking a spin doctor to clean up his triple-X image and sell him as
a high-minded politician, after he was Morganed by playful Piers.'

'Cleggover' had a rather inevitable feel to it, as did the comparisons with
the **Paddy Pantsdown** headlines, harking back to an earlier Lib Dem
leader Paddy Ashdown and the news of an extra-marital affair. Both
names demonstrate the kind of wordplay at which newspapers have
become so successful. 'Will **Hillzilla** crush **Obambi**?' was the heading in
The New York Times in December 2006 as the presidential nomination
race kicked off.

The creation of nicknames for politicians has a long and successful history.
Some epithets have had an affectionate feel to them – as the Lib Dems
claimed was the case for Clegg – while many have distilled everything
about a person that the electorate dislikes. **Milk-Snatcher** was applied to
Margaret Thatcher when free milk in schools was ended on her watch as
Education Minister; in her time she was also given the epithets **Attila the
Hen**, **Tina** (There Is No Alternative), and of course **the Iron Lady**. **Two
Jags** was the label given to former Deputy Prime Minister John Prescott

while he was Environment Minister and owner of two government cars (prompting the then opposition leader William Hague to remark that Prescott's 'idea of a park-and-ride scheme is to park one Jaguar so that he can ride away in the other'). Tony Blair was initially nicknamed **Bambi** thanks to his youth and relative inexperience. It did not last long, and it was for a time replaced by **Stalin**, long before that name was levelled at his then Chancellor Gordon Brown.

Many politicians have embraced the nicknames created for them. **The Iron Chancellor** was almost self-appointed and carried deliberate echoes of Otto von Bismarck (rather than, presumably, Mrs Thatcher, who also relished 'the Iron Lady'). Bill Clinton actually coined **the Comeback Kid** for himself, when he failed to win what was then seen as the crucial New Hampshire primary but vowed to go on to win. **Supermac**, the name given to the Prime Minister Harold Macmillan by the cartoonist Vicky (Victor Weisz), was intended to be derisive, but Macmillan turned it to his advantage and it soon became an integral part of his political identity.

The current British PM has attracted a wealth of nicknames since his accession to the political throne. After his decision not to hold an election he became known as **Bottler Brown**, whilst the Liberal Democrats dubbed him as the incompetent **Mr Bean** (later to become **Mr Has-Been**). Most recent quips at his expense include 'fiddler on the hoof' and, suggested by Fraser Nelson at *The Spectator* in a neat allusion to Margaret Thatcher's own words, 'the laddie is for turning'.

cripes

a (dated) expression of surprise or dismay.

The exclamation '**Cripes**!' has all the resonance of a *Beano* or St Trinian's character: it is now rather sweetly old-fashioned, and confers an air of naivety on the speaker. This last attribute perhaps came in useful for one very distinctive politician: in 2008 'cripes' became the trademark of the Conservative MP Boris Johnson's successful bid for the mayorship of London.

Johnson, one of the few politicians to be identified by his first name alone, is one of the most recognizable figures in modern British politics. Journalists have this down to his trademark unruly hair and bumbling gait, together with a highly individual style of speaking – at times remarkably blunt, at others deliberately circuitous. All three traits of what has been dubbed 'Homo Johnsoniensis' have made their bearer a ripe target for satirists. 'Cripes', whether or not Johnson utters it as much as the media pretends, is entirely in keeping with his self-styled wide-eyed manner and the occasional act of the blundering buffoon and toff.

Countless headlines confirmed that 'cripes' had indeed become a trademark term:

'Cripes! Boris Johnson reveals he's a serious buffer after all.' (*The Times*, 14 March 2008.)

' "Affordable housing – erm, cripes, yes, we'll do something about that too".' (*The Telegraph*, 4 April 2008.)

When the mayoral election had been fought and won, *The Independent* found 'cripes' a useful summary for a whole lot more than one politician's victory: 'Cripes! Boris takes London (and rounds off a rotten day for Gordon Brown)'.

'**C**ripes' is a euphemistic alteration of 'Christ': the *Oxford English Dictionary*'s first record of it is from a 1910 novel and in the form of 'By cripes!'. If it was once a means of avoiding profanity, it is now a term packed with resonances of schoolboy larks in times past.

There are many other terms, like 'cripes', which have their roots in a religious phrase – or in its avoidance. **Crikey**, too, is a euphemism for 'Christ', and goes back to the 1830s.

Looking even further back, this time to the 16th century at least, is the term **gramercy**. An anglicization of the Old French *grant merci*, and used to mean 'thank you', 'gramercy' is recorded from Middle English onwards. Samuel Johnson, in his Dictionary of 1755, believed the term to have a slightly different origin: from 'grant me mercy', and so he defined it as an exclamation of surprise – 'mercy on us!' Probably as a result of his interpretation, 'gramercy' was picked up in the 19th century, usually in consciously archaic writing such as Coleridge's *Rime of the Ancient Mariner*: 'Gramercy! They for joy did grin.'

Marry was a variant of 'Mary', recorded from Middle English on. Again it was used as one of the many euphemisms of religious oaths, in this case for 'By Mary'. Oliver Goldsmith's *The Vicar of Wakefield* of 1766 includes the line 'Marry, hang the ideot. . . . to bring me such stuff'.

The word **jingo** emerged in the late 17th century as a piece of conjuror's talk (rather like 'hey presto'), but it soon established itself as a means of asserting something vigorously. It was with such emphatic delivery that the famous 1878 music-hall song by G. W. Hunt used it, in reference to the Russian-Turkish war and Russia's threat to Constantinople: 'We don't want to fight, yet by Jingo! if we do. . . . We've got the ships, we've got the men, and got the money too!'

Thanks to the song, the word 'jingoism' was born. London's *Daily News* was one of the first to use the term when it called those who were against Russian interests 'jingoes' in its issue of 11 March 1878. Two days later a subscriber wrote to the paper about 'the Jingoes – the new type of music-hall patriots who sing the Jingo song'. Few who use that term today to describe a bellicose chauvinistic attitude to foreigners would realize its history.

Gadzooks is another in the list of old-fashioned exclamations which would seldom be used today without some conscious reference to a period in the past: in this case the 18th century. Tobias Smollett included it in the wonderfully-titled *The Adventures of Peregrine Pickle* in 1751, when the word was at the height of its popularity: ' "What!" cried the painter, in despair, "become a singer? Gadzooks! and the devil and all that! I'll rather be still where I am, and let myself be devoured by vermin." '

'Gadzooks' is usually said to be an alteration of 'God's hooks', that is, the nails by which Christ was fastened to the cross. The linguist Michael Quinion, in his website *World Wide Words*, adds yet more words to the euphemistic list of oaths from the late 17th and early 18th centuries that used 'gad' as a thinly disguised version of 'God', among them **Gadsbobs**, **Gadsnigs**, **Gadsbudlikins**, **Gadsokers**, **Gadsprecious**, and **Gadswookers**.

cybrid

a hybrid cell produced artificially to create a human-animal embryo (a blend of 'cytoplasmic' + 'hybrid').

The word **cybrid** dates back as far as 1974. It is essentially an embryo formed by injecting a human cell nucleus into an empty animal egg. The DNA of the resulting cell would be 99.9% human.

Although around for some time, 'cybrid' hit the headlines in April 2008 when it was announced, as in the *Telegraph* on 1 April 2008, that 'the first hybrid embryos in Europe – a blend of human and cow DNA – have been created by scientists in Newcastle'. The aim of such creations is to enable better research into diseases such as diabetes and Parkinson's.

The report sparked off a heated debate on ethics, with opponents utilizing terms such as 'Frankenstein creations' and 'chimeras' (see below). Headlines – and there were many – were often a mixture of alarm and humour. The *New Scientist* announced: 'Cybrids are go . . . but what will come home to roost?', while the website *momlogic* pondered the prospect of 'Having a Cow . . . Literally'.

If the doors were partly opened to cybrids, it remained closed to **chimeras**, embryos that contain both human and animal cells.

The word 'chimera' originally referred to the fabled fire-breathing monster of Greek mythology which bore a lion's head, a goat's body, and a serpent's tail. It is first recorded in English in the 14th century in Wyclif's Bible, and is one of many animal hybrids in classical and other mythologies. Beyond its original point of reference, the word has endured in figurative language where it means, to quote the *Oxford English Dictionary*, 'an unreal creature of the imagination, a mere wild fancy; an unfounded conception': a sense which evolved as early as the late 1500s.

The 'literal' definition of a grotesque monster, formed of the parts of human monsters, was resurrected with the beginning of chimeric experimentation. This process, seen by some as the cutting edge of the biotech revolution, involves the combination of genetic material from different species, or human and animal cells, in one creature. The intention behind such research is to create animals which are similar to humans in their genetic make-up, and to therefore provide more accurate models of how diseases develop. In 2005, one potential result of such experimentation was the **humanzee**, a proposed combination of human and chimpanzee material in the same organism.

The implications of producing such creatures became a matter of vociferous debate, with critics warning that its moral and legal status would throw thousands of years of ethics into chaos. A 'cybrid' sounds (perhaps because of 'cyborg') rooted in science fiction. While that clearly isn't the case, the term and the phenomenon looked this year to be very far from becoming ordinary.

data exhaust

1. information stored on our computer hard drive and online as a result of our Internet activities.
2. inconsequential information passed between members of social networking sites.

As more and more of us perform our daily activities online, so the trail of digital footprints gets bigger, exposing in the process increasing amounts of information about us. This is information we may not want others to share, but which is the inevitable consequence of our online activity. Then there is the information that we *do* want to share, however insignificant, via *Facebook* or *Twitter* and other networking sites.

Both categories of information have been referred to as **data exhaust**: rather than gas or air, the output is photos, blogs, videos, chat messages, and more. For some, it might yet be pollution, albeit of the virtual kind. For others, however, it is clearly an essential ingredient of communicating in the digital age.

drawdown

a reduction in the size or presence of a military force.

At a press conference at the close of 2006, President Bush announced his administration's new strategy for Iraq, the thrust of which was likely to be an increase in the number of troops sent to Baghdad. The term the President used for the increased presence of US forces was **surge**, the successor to the word **escalation** associated with Vietnam. **Drawdown**, meanwhile, is the military antithesis, denoting the downsizing of troop numbers as a run-up to a complete withdrawal.

Although this specific sense of 'drawdown' has been around for a time, it was Bill Clinton who brought it into the spotlight in 2007 when he warned in an interview on National Public Radio that keeping high troop levels in place could hurt US interests:

'I think for our own national security we almost have no choice but to have substantial troop drawdown in Iraq this year because we already have badly overstressed the Army, the Marine Corps, the Guard and the Reserves. If we had a genuine national security emergency in this country tomorrow that required ground forces, they would have to be supplied by the Navy and the Air Force.'

For proponents of a speedy drawdown the news in the early months of 2008 was disappointing. Concerns that recent security gains could backslide meant that President Bush looked likely to leave his successor the same number of troops as at 'presurge' levels.

For all their destruction, wars, paradoxically, have a generative effect on language. Each major war has spawned new vocabulary: World War I produced **shell-shocked** and **no-man's land**, while World War II saw the coinages **Jeep** (made from the initials *GP*, for general purpose, and probably influenced by the character of Eugene the Jeep, a creature of amazing power first introduced in the *Popeye* cartoon strip) and **firestorm**.

The Second Gulf War was no exception. New terms, or new senses of older ones, required daily glossaries in national newspapers as readers endeavoured to keep up. **Embeds** was the new term for journalists who lived the war alongside the soldiers, while **weapons of mass destruction**, **mouseholing** (blowing an entry hole in the wall of an enemy building rather than risking a booby-trapped door), and **blue-on-blue** (the successor to the equally euphemistic 'friendly fire') also cemented themselves in the language thanks to their guaranteed exposure. As well as battle codenames, such as **Desert Storm**, **Infinite Justice**, and **Enduring Freedom**, unofficial signature terms emerged too. If **mother of all battles** became a distillation of the First Gulf war, then **shock and awe** became the phrase for the Second.

And, of course, the **war on terror**, as well as the stated justification for a whole new set of military strategies, has also seen a new lexicon of warfare grow up around it.

earmarxist

a member of Congress who adds earmarks (money designated for pet projects) to legislation.

In US political parlance, an **earmark** is money allocated in a spending bill for specific projects. The term takes its image from the earmarking of livestock as a means of identification and allocation to the owning farmer. An earmark can be part of legislation (a 'hard earmark'), which makes the spending of the money on that particular cause legally binding, or it can be a recommendation within a committee bill, known as a 'soft earmark'.

It is standard practice for legislators to insert earmarks for projects within their own home state. Senator Hillary Clinton, for example, was reported by the online political journal *The Hill* to have requested nearly $2.3 billion dollars' worth of federal earmarks for 2009, while Senator Barack Obama was said to have decided to spurn earmarks and to seek no funds for pet projects for the forthcoming year.

The coining of the term **earmarxist** has been claimed by the Republican blog *Redstate* as a specific term for Democrats who opposed funding earmarked for the continuing war effort in Iraq and Afghanistan. In March 2007, one blogger commented: 'I can't help but think we should be calling anti-war porkers in Congress "Earmarxists." ' The linguistic inspiration was in response to an op-ed piece from *The Wall Street Journal* on a bill requesting more funding for the troops:

'This bill has everything the modern military doesn't need. There's $25 million for spinach, designed to attract the vote of Sam Farr, a California farm-region liberal. Perhaps spinach growers who lost business due to last year's

21

E. coli scare need this taxpayer bailout, but it won't intimidate the Taliban unless Mr. Farr plans to draft Popeye.'

(A very different kind of 'green' mentality, perhaps.)

'**E**armarxist' was picked up by *The New York Times* later in 2007 and named one of their 'buzzwords' of the year. If it proves to be no more than a passing sarcasm, it nonetheless demonstrates the power of today's political blog.

Earmarks are an established – if controversial – part of the US political system. In 2007, political blogs and chat forums were full of such bewildering statements as 'Earmarxist perfectly describes the process of taking money from you and giving it back to you as a pork barrel.'

A **pork barrel** is a political metaphor for the utilization of government funds in a way that benefits certain constituents or party donors: the result is more votes, and more funds. The term is said to date from before the Civil War, when Southern slave-owners, in their more charitable moments, would make a gift to their slaves of salt pork. The pork would be put out in a barrel at a set time on an announced day, and the slaves would rush to it and take what they could. As a result, a pork barrel was seen as a 'gift' of appeasement.

In one of his celebrated *Letter from America* broadcasts, Alistair Cooke explained pork barrelling as an annual process in which an extraordinarily lengthy bill, containing hundreds of 'pet causes', is put forward to the House: 'So, many a lulu, lemon or what the 19th century called a "screamer" gets through. I'm sure nobody's going to deny the State of Maine a request in favour of more research on blueberries since it's a useful part of the State's economy.'

Both pork barrels and earmark politics have become associated with a variety of colourful legislative terms. Among them is **Christmas tree bills**. When members of Congress add their own 'pork barrel' amendments, these special projects are seen to be hung upon a bill in the same way as ornaments and baubles adorn a Christmas tree.

And then there is **logrolling**, whereby members trade their votes to support each other's projects. The origin is again an agricultural one: namely the frontier practice of neighbouring farmers helping each other gather logs for house-building and fencing. Whoever helped his neighbour with logrolling would be helped in return. (**Blogrolling** is today's online version.)

Political metaphors are not always easily translatable. As Alistair Cooke put it in that 2003 broadcast:

'The dictionary gives an accurate but prim definition of "pork barrel" – "appropriations secured by Congressmen for local projects." That's about as enlightening as defining a dictatorship as a "system of government whereby one man is in control of the main branches".'

ecotown

communities which rely on renewable energy for their power and which aspire to be carbon-neutral. Part of Gordon Brown's vision for 21st-century Britain is the creation of several experimental 'ecotowns'.

While the word **ecotown** is not new, it has gained considerable currency in 2008, both as part of our daily discussions of carbon footprints, and as a result of some controversy about the ecotown's objectives.

First the term itself. In becoming an ecotown, a community signs up to several objectives for sustainable living. These are not just ecological, but also embrace values of social justice and community involvement. There are many precedents in North America and in Europe, in particular Sweden, where the non-profit organization The Natural Step has pioneered the sustainable town. Ecotowns are known by the alternative name of **eco municipalities** and have the stated aim of meeting human needs in a way that is fair to the environment.

In February 2008, protesters demonstrated near the site of a proposed ecotown in Warwickshire, arguing that there had been insufficient local consultation and that the scheme was a government excuse for building new homes in inappropriate places such as greenfield sites.

Certainly, the protesters would have it, the name 'ecotown' specifically tries to use a positive term to conceal what they would believe to be a negative fact. 'Ecotown' and **green veneer** are proving to be a regular linguistic pairing.

If **footprint** is fast becoming one of the most versatile nouns of the decade, so **eco-** is one of its most productive prefixes, and it has been so for a surprisingly long time. The form 'eco-' detached itself from its parent 'ecology' as early as 1969, when terms such as **eco-catastrophe**, **eco-freak**, and **eco-activist** can be found. Not much later came **eco-nut**, **eco-terrorism**, **eco-doom**, **eco-warrior**, and even **eco-porn**: corporate advertisements boasting environmental concern that may or may not be borne out in its practices.

If the proliferation of 'eco-' words has diluted some of its impact, it had until recently largely escaped the sometimes contentious associations of 'green' (as in the recently coined **greenwashing** for environmentalist 'whitewashing'). Today, however, combinations which include it are not always overwhelmingly positive: take **eco-mafia**, for example, or **eco-babble**. Leo Hickman, writing in *The Guardian*, commented in early 2008 that 'the "eco" tag seems to be fast losing its lustre [. . .] Most of us have watched an episode of *Grand Designs* in which we follow the construction of an "eco house" only to watch as the owner ends up using tonnes of concrete because an "eco" construction material would require them taking out a third mortgage, let alone a second.'

Good or bad, one thing for certain is that 'eco-' has proved linguistically remarkable in its versatility. The *Oxford English Dictionary* lists almost a hundred terms which have 'eco' as their prefix. 'Ecotown' alone has been joined by the **eco village**, **eco city**, and **ecopolis**.

While at the beginning of the new millennium the explosion of online vocabulary was fully expected, not every linguist would have predicted the extent to which environmental matters would influence the lexicon of the noughties. The first eight years have seen the prolific 'greening' of our language. The phrase 'reduce our footprint' today requires no glossing, and indeed those footprints come in many forms, whether carbon or ecological, economic or industrial. At the beginning of the 2000s, the evidence of the Oxford English Corpus, a vast database of
recorded current language, is that 'carbon' and 'ecological' featured

rarely on the linguistic map for 'footprint': today they are among its most frequent companions, along with the imperative to 'reduce'.

'Green' and 'eco' may well emerge at the end of the century as the supreme prefixes of their time.

embuggerance

a terrible nuisance; a source of irritation or frustration.

The world of Terry Pratchett is an absurd and fantastical one, full of illogicalities. Best known for his series of fantasy novels set on 'Discworld', a planet shaped like a pizza which floats through the universe carried by four elephants who themselves are standing on a giant turtle, the author announced in December 2007 that he was suffering from a rare form of early onset Alzheimer's disease. His announcement, posted on the website of his illustrator Paul Kidby, was entitled simply 'An **Embuggerance**'.

The downplaying of such devastating news did little to lessen its impact. The choice of the word 'embuggerance' was a powerful one, entirely at home with Pratchett's humour and resonant of the world of *Monty Python* on which the author is said to draw.

The word itself dates back over half a century. The slang chronicler Eric Partridge included the extended term 'embuggerance factor' in his *Dictionary of Slang and Unconventional English*, defining it as 'a natural or artificial hazard that complicates any proposed course of action'. 'Embuggerance' clearly draws on the terms 'bugger' and 'buggering about', both of which (but particularly the latter which has an affectionate, even old-fashioned feel to it) are less taboo today than they once were. 'Embuggerance' itself has been largely restricted to military use but has crossed over into general use, such as in 2001 when *The Guardian* quoted the novelist Louis de Bernières: 'In fact, he has had to put up with so much "brainless and trivial embuggerance", he says, that he has come to regret having written Corelli in the first place.'

Terry Pratchett's widely-reported use of the word will undoubtedly widen its audience, albeit in very sad circumstances.

'Embuggerance' has all the feel of a fictional creation by such writers as Edward Lear and Lewis Carroll, who invented words such as **runcible spoon**, **crumbobblious**, **fizzgiggious**, and **scroobious** (Lear) and **brillig**, **gimble**, **mimsy**, **galumph**, and **jabberwocky** (Carroll). It could equally be at home in the animated world of *The Simpsons*, where wordplay is all, and produces such novelties as 'a noble spirit **embiggens** the smallest man'.

'Embuggerance' is, as the critic Bryan Appleyard put it, 'a fine word'. He added, 'and a fine spirit is behind it.'

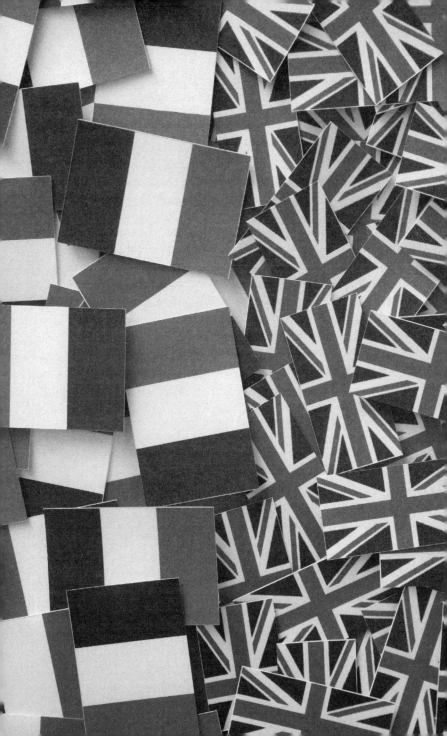

entente amicale

(French) an amicable relationship.

The phrase **entente amicale** was suggested by the new President of France Nicolas Sarkozy as a replacement for the long-established 'entente cordiale' (literally, 'a cordial understanding') during a visit to Britain in March 2008.

The original **entente cordiale** was a series of agreements between Britain and France signed in April 1904. It signalled the end of centuries of conflict between the two countries that culminated in Napoleon's wars, and heralded the World War alliance between the two biggest European democracies against Germany. In the centenary year of the Entente, 2004, and in spite of the Queen's announcement 'Vive la différence, mais vive l'entente cordiale', Britons and the French were said to hold more enmity towards each other than friendship. France's decision not to support the British and American offensives against Iraq put the relationship under further pressure, resulting in an exchange of insults including the now famous 'cheese-eating surrender monkeys', borrowed from an episode of *The Simpsons* and widely picked up by the media as the conflict began.

Nicolas Sarkozy's wry reference to a relationship that has at times been highly strained, and his suggestion of an upgrade to something warmer, prompted hopes in the optimistic of a closer Anglo-French alliance. For those more cynical, there remained cause for doubt. The *Financial Times* observed that 'the history of Anglo-French relations is littered with grand promises of fresh starts that quickly turn mouldy'.

During the President's first visit, however, amicability showed no signs of decay. Gordon Brown topped the list of variations on a theme with his conclusion that the future relationship was going to be an **entente formidable**.

31

ethicurean

a person who eats and drinks according to their moral and ethical principles.

The food blog *The Ethicurean* carries the slogan 'Chew the right thing'. The website, dedicated to the eating of sustainable foods, defines the eponymous term as 'someone who seeks out tasty things that are also sustainable, organic, local and/or ethical – SOLE food for short'.

The **ethicurean**'s choices are informed by a complex set of concerns, not all of which are compatible. While some principles are simple – for example, the more processed a food is, the more energy it has cost to produce it – other questions are hotly debated by those who strive to follow their conscience: should, for example, third-world workers be supported even if many food-miles are covered in order to bring the results of their efforts to our plates? Navigating the modern food landscape is a challenge: one *The Sydney Morning Herald* recently described as 'a moral minefield of complex issues centred on the size of our foodie footprint'.

Even *The Simpsons* have been doing some soul-searching. In the episode 'Apocalypse Cow' Bart unexpectedly (for someone who can't become a vegetarian because he 'loves the taste of death' too much) feels sympathy for a cow he names Lou. When the steer is sent to a 'feedlot' for factory farming, Lisa and her vegan activist friends help Bart to rescue it. The episode has been celebrated by ethicureans for its raising of issues such as corn subsidies, cattle growth hormones, and slaughterhouse practices: as one blogger put it, under the inevitable headline 'Apocalypse Cowabunga!': 'Well, it doesn't have GMOs or evil food capitalists, but luckily those get covered in the classic tomacco episode . . . Oh, "Simpsons." Is there any food politics issue you can't enlighten us on?'

exergame

a video game that requires the player(s) to make physical movements and so gain exercise.

Blends are not always the most elegant of word-creations, and **exergame** is no exception. Its predecessor **exertainment** has been around since the early 2000s, used to describe the latest gadgetry, iPods, and TV screens offered by gyms to tempt the faint-hearted. 'Exergame' itself has been around, although not in any great currency, since 2005, but it is with the advent of the **Wii** that the concept has really come into its own. The video game console, unveiled in 2005, allows players to participate in games in a physical way, achieving a 'controlled workout' in the process.

The exergame is able to track full body movements in three dimensions, monitoring speed, reaction time, and strength. The latest consoles incorporate motion sensors such as accelerometers and gyroscopes that are used to direct the player's behaviour within the game.

Whether it's football, offroading, baseball, boxing, aerobics, ski jumping, or rowing, 'exertainment' is seen by some as the key to tackling the **globesity** epidemic.

Such is the success of the Wii, it has spawned a set of linguistic as well as commercial spin-offs. Its motion-sensitive remote control is called, of course, the **Wiimote**, while the resulting physical workout has given rise to the terms **Wiiflexes**, and **Wii elbow**: arm pain caused by excessive use. Further 'Wii-' compounds are only to be expected.

exoplanet

a planet outside our solar system.

On 20 March 2008, the scientific journal *Nature* published evidence that an organic molecule had been found on an extrasolar planet for the first time. Although water vapour had, a year earlier, been detected in the spectrum of one previously discovered **exoplanet**, the new analyses showed not only water vapour but also the existence of methane in the atmosphere of the giant gas planet.

While conditions on 'HD 189733 b' are too harsh to enable life, it is the first time a key molecule for organic life has been found on an extrasolar planet. One month earlier, astronomers had announced that a miniature version of our own solar system had been discovered, 5,000 light years across the galaxy. *The New York Times* of 15 February quoted Sara Seager, a theorist at the Massachusetts Institute of Technology: 'Right now in exoplanets we are on an inexorable path to finding other Earths.' She praised the discovery as 'a big step in finding out if our planetary system is alone'.

One result of such important steps forward is that the term 'exoplanet' has been propelled back into wider currency. It joins other terms from the field of space exploration that have been harnessed by a wider public in recent years, thanks in part to our necessarily increasing awareness of the environmental threats facing our own planet.

Despite our best efforts to be eco-savvy, many fear that we may have already damaged our own planet beyond repair, as signalled by the so-called **climate canaries** of cyclones, earthquakes, and floods that have in very recent times produced tragic numbers of **climate refugees**. **Global dimming**, because each year less light reaches the surface of the Earth as a result of increases in black carbon and other particulates in the atmosphere, is also thought to be the direct result of human activity.

As a consequence, the quest for a **Goldilocks planet** whose size, temperature, and composition (like the porridge of the story's three bears) are all favourable to life continues. We should hope that the newly-discovered exoplanets are not **plutoed**: a verb that came into (and quickly fell out of) currency in 2006 following the demotion of the planet Pluto to what was termed a dwarf planet or 'planemo'. If the direst climate change predictions prove not to be eco-scams, we may need to visit it.

facebook (verb)

1. to look for details about someone using the *Facebook* website, a social networking site on which friends exchange messages and photos.
2. to communicate with someone via the *Facebook* website.

The *Facebook* site was established in 2004 by the American IT guru Mark Zuckerberg. It has proved a phenomenal success, with a membership today totalling over 60 million. It was therefore only a matter of time before, like Google before it, it acquired linguistic success and became a formulation in itself. To **facebook** can be used in several ways. To facebook another person is to check out their personal space on the site or to send them a message. Indeed, if Google is the model for the term, it seems likely that more meanings for 'facebooking' will emerge, and that compounds will be coined in the manner of **Googlewhacking** (the quest to find a two-word search that delivers just one result from the Google search engine) or **Googlebooking** (to search for something in Google's digitized book collection: see page 49).

Online communities tend to generate their own vocabularies – eBay, for example, has seen a whole bidding and selling lexicon grow up around it. Facebooking is no exception. Several terms specific to *Facebook* communication have been coined. The verbs **pimp** and **poke**, for example, have acquired new senses. To **pimp** one's space on the site is to enhance it via the addition of photographs, graphics, or music, while to **poke** a fellow member is to prompt them to communicate, or to nudge them into giving attention (as a result it frequently has sexual overtones, and is beginning to crop up in general language as such).

See also SLEEVEFACING.

femtocell

a base station in the home for a mobile phone.

The term **femtocell** has been familiar to those working within the telecommunications industry for some time, but it has largely flown below the radar in the outside world. In 2008, developments were announced which looked set to change all that.

The femtocell's base station can be set up as an adjunct to a home's broadband Internet service. The idea is to give subscribers both a better signal and faster data access, as reception in buildings using traditional technology is often poor. Using a femtocell, a person's mobile phone can be the primary point of contact within the home as it is outside and in the office.

The femtocell may well have other benefits too, namely an extended battery life given the low signal levels required – an advance which may also mitigate fears of adverse health effects. Phone companies hope that femtocells will encourage people to use the high-speed data services that have been introduced at huge cost and will help to draw users away from their competitors, the fixed-line telecoms operators. Products are appearing at trade shows but have yet to go on retail sale.

The word itself has been coined using the prefix 'femto-', from Danish or Norwegian 'femten' meaning fifteen and which in this case means 10^{-15} or one quadrillionth (a million billionth) of a unit, and 'cell', short for 'cellular radio'. The term is already being widely abbreviated to 'femto' in the telecoms business.

flame attendant

the name given by the Beijing Organizing Committee
for the Olympic Games to security guards from China's
People's Armed Police, who accompanied the runners
carrying the traditional Olympic torch during its journey
around the world.

*T*he *Guardian* called it 'the world's most guarded relay': the
procession of the Olympic torch around London and other
world cities to mark the run-up to the 2008 Games in China was
anything but a 'Journey of Harmony', its chosen theme. The protest
against the host nation's human rights violations, and particularly
against its treatment of Tibet, gathered momentum at each
successive stage of the relay. Such was the threatened – and, in cities
such as Paris, very real – unrest that the torch was twice extinguished
and transported by bus to its next destination. (The flame itself is
maintained in a back-up lantern which is used to reignite the torch
when necessary.)

The term **flame attendant** was notable for its note of
officialdom, particularly when compared to 'torch-bearer', a
concept steeped in historical and literary tradition. Observers of the
torch relay in London, witnessing skirmishes between the attendants
and the police, started to question what authority they held within
Britain. According to the Metropolitan Police, they had none.

Headlines such as 'China sends in clowns' and 'Up in flames'
ran above stories of Beijing's humiliation. John Lichfield,
writing in *The Independent*, reported back from Paris: 'In theory,
the torch was to be sealed from public and protesters by a security
cordon 200m long. A phalanx of 100 roller-skating policemen
guarded one flank and 100 jogging firemen defended the other.

As in London, Chinese flame attendants in bright blue tracksuits surrounded the torch-bearer . . . Instead of a celebration of China's emergence as a world power, the journey of the flame has turned into a trail of shame.'

Officially, Beijing has said only that the mission of the '29th Olympic Games Torch Relay Flame Protection Unit' was to guard the flame in keeping with the practice of past Olympic Games. Members were picked from special police units of the People's Armed Police, China's internal security force. According to the state-run China News Service, the requirements for the job were as follows: 'tall, handsome, mighty, in exceptional physical condition similar to that of professional athletes'.

Such physical prowess was viewed rather differently in the West to the East. Denounced as 'thugs' and paramilitary goons by Western commentators, in China the flame attendants became heroes. None more so, it seemed, than one young tracksuit-clad security guard stationed to the right of the torch carriers and dubbed 'second right brother' by legions of Chinese fans.

freeconomics

the business practice of giving away goods or services as a means of gaining new business or retaining existing customers.

The term **freeconomics** was coined by Chris Anderson in an essay published in *Wired* magazine called 'The Long Tail' (a term he also created to describe the niche strategy of certain retailers who profit from the cumulative volume effect of small sales).

In his article, Anderson quotes the computer scientist Carver Mead: ' "What happens when things get (nearly) free?" His answer is that you waste them, be they transistors or megabytes of bandwidth capacity. . . . You do crazy things like offering people the ability to put their whole music collection in their pocket, or promising the average email user that they'll never have to delete another message to conserve space. . . . With apologies to Levitt and Dubner, I'll cheekily call the emerging realization that abundance is driving our world "freeconomics".'

The reality of freeconomics – the free exchange of goods and services, particularly over the Web – is seen by many experts as a threat to traditional economies and corporations that have been built on private ownership. The giveaways are of course not without their own aim: if something is offered free, as one commentator puts it, 'you are halfway there to hooking that fish'.

Chris Anderson's reference to Steven Levitt and Stephen Dubner gives the clue to his coinage. 'Freeconomics' is his alternative to **freakonomics**, Levitt and Dubner's term in their application of economic theory to subjects as diverse as sumo wrestling and naming children (in a book which was number two on the *New York Times* Bestseller List and which to date has sold over 3 million copies worldwide).

The linguistic spin-offs from economics have been almost as numerous as the physical and theoretical ones. In recent decades we have seen:

attention economics: an economic model that is premised on the attention span of the individual consumer even as the information bandwidth continues to widen.

ecolonomics: ecologically- and environmentally-minded economic practice.

econophysics: the application of physics to economic models.

womenomics: a model that reflects the increasing role that women are playing in economic growth.

Enronomics: business practice that is based on dodgy or fraudulent accounting practices, as in the case of the US energy company Enron which collapsed in spectacular fashion in 2001.

cappuccino economy: an economy that demonstrates rapid growth in one area while only steady or slow growth in its other sectors.

Finally, there is the **Goldilocks economy**, beautifully described on Paul McFedries' *Word Spy* website as 'an economy that is not so overheated that it causes inflation, and not so cool that it causes a recession'.

freemale

an unmarried woman.

Marketing companies are often responsible for the strangest of coinages. More often than not they are designed to create instant publicity rather than any lasting addition to our language, and **freemale**, yet another term invented for a particular and newly defined demographic, is surely one of them.

The term first appeared in Australia in the spring of 2008. It followed a survey conducted by a database marketing company, the outcome of which was the statistic that unmarried women now outnumber married women down under for the first time since World War I. The report, entitled 'Bridget Jones meets Sex and the City', invented the even clumsier acronym **SPUD**, for a 'single person urban dwelling'.

However tongue-in-cheek the coinages, not everyone reacted in the same way. A columnist for the Australian *Daily Telegraph* responded with her own creation: **AOBWRTASIALBJ** (Angry Old Bag Who Refuses To Accept She Is Anything Like Bridget Jones).

The marketing theory behind PR campaigns which use a fictional coinage as their springboard is that people like new words. New words are connected with new ideas, and if one can be made fashionable, it is bound to be picked up by the public at large who will, unwittingly, also pay commercial dividends by buying the product with which it is associated.

Such was the theory in 2004 when the Fremont Company of Ohio launched a campaign to promote the increased consumption of its 'Franks Kraut' brand of sauerkraut. The hook of its message was the **k'tini**: a 'kraut martini' with the essential ingredient of two olives stuffed with sauerkraut floating in a cloudy pool of gin.

The following year, one US company tried to sell family vacations by pushing the concept of **togethering**, which it defined as 'the new trend of traveling together with friends or colleagues to a destination'. **Ant hill family**, meanwhile – the coinage of another PR department – purported to name the trend wherein children move back in with their parents so that all work together toward group financial goals.

None of these terms survived much longer than the campaigns that propelled them, briefly, into the public domain. Arguably they were never used without direct reference to the efforts of that particular company.

Force-fed coinages of this kind stand even less chance of succeeding than words that have emerged organically. Exceptions to the rule – **va va voom** surely exceeded all of Renault's expectations by becoming an idiom unto itself – survive in spite of the obstacles facing them. 'Freemale' is likely to go with the majority rule and to disappear without trace. Perhaps the pollsters should have stuck with **quirkyalone**, coined in 2000 to define a happy singleton and a word that clearly has the edge over other wannabe neologisms.

free range kid

a child who is allowed lots of unstructured time for play and other self-chosen activities during the day.

In his book *Under Pressure: Rescuing Childhood from the Culture of Hyper-Parenting*, the Canadian philosopher and writer Carl Honoré promotes the idea of freedom for children as part of his belief in the 'slow movement': a cultural ethos which advocates slowing down the pace of our lives. If we take a step back and question the value of organizing every second of our children's lives, we might well find the free-range parenting option a far more productive one.

In a piece for *The New York Sun*, Lenore Skenazy raised some controversy by admitting she allows her 9-year-old child to use the New York subway. As a result of the ensuing debate, in which Skenazy was both applauded and condemned, the columnist set up a blog entitled *Free Range Kids*, which emphasizes the value of giving children the same freedoms that today's adults themselves enjoyed in their childhood. In other words, the aim is to buck the trend of the **helicopter mom** – who hovers over her child incessantly. Intensive farming versus free-range rearing: the choice may for many be much harder to make when it comes to children than to food.

frogamander

the pet name coined for the fossil Gerobatrachus hottoni ('Hotton's elderly frog') (blend of 'frog' + 'salamander').

The announcement in May that a 290 million-year-old fossil may yet complete a missing link in the history of fossils provided much excitement, and not just because of its name. Gerobatrachus, dubbed a **frogamander** because of its mixture of frog and salamander features, was discovered in Texas back in 1995 and was painstakingly removed from layers of rock.

The results of the ensuing study suggest that frogs and salamanders do, as suspected, indeed share a common ancestry. The fossil showed the fused ankle bones seen only in salamanders but a wide, frog-like skull. Its backbone resembles a mix of the two.

The scientist leading the study, Jason Anderson from the University of Calgary, declared the fossil to be a 'perfect little frogamander'. His quip may yet be the source of one of the most resilient words of the year.

glamping

camping in luxury (blend of 'glamorous' + 'camping').

Glamping, so *The Sunday Times* announced in the summer of 2007, is 'camping's more glamorous twin. It's time to upgrade.' Fed up with the treacheries of British weather and sodden sleeping bags, and eager to embrace the reassurance of a low carbon footprint but not that of a double bed, glamping is a heady mix of fresh air and comfort. As Tiffanie Darke continues in her account of her transformation from camper to glamper: '**Glampers** donate their roll mats to the boy scouts. For them, sheepskin rugs, leather pouffes, chilled champagne boxes, silk- and muslin-strewn gazebos, Egyptian-cotton sheets, blow-up sofas, double duvets – even tea-light chandeliers – are all part of the alfresco setup.'

Glamping is characterized by its accessories. Tents are of the five-metre waterproof kind, boast Velcro windows and, as one advertisement has it (calling it 'camping with soul'), a canopy which can double up as a 'spectacular chill-out area for a summer garden party'. In a vivid description of a luxury camping resort in Montana, the *Los Angeles Times* lists some of the perks of glamping it up: 'a camp butler to build their fire, a maid to crank up the heated down comforter at nightfall and a cook to whip up bison rib-eye for dinner and French toast topped with huckleberries for breakfast'. The paper also notes an alternative term for such cushioned camping, used in all sincerity by the travel companies which offer it – **soft adventure**.

God's access

an apparent codeword within the Secret Intelligence Service, MI6, for permission to search its files.

2008 saw the conclusion of the inquest into the deaths of Princess Diana and Dodi Fayed in August 1997. On 7 April the jury decided that the couple had been unlawfully killed as a result of the negligent driving of their chauffeur, Henri Paul, and of paparazzi photographers who had set off in pursuit of them.

The day after the verdict was announced, *The Times* published a summary of the key moments and people involved in the events which led to Princess Diana's death and those which followed. This included a person described by the paper as a real-life 'Miss Moneypenny', known only as Miss X, who gave evidence on camera. She gave details of her 25 years of service to MI6, and of how, for the purposes of the inquest, she had been temporarily given **God's access**: or permission to search the complete records kept by the Service. This privilege was normally restricted to the Director of MI6 and his deputy.

As it turned out, Miss X found no files at all on the Princess, but she did find one on Mohamed Al Fayed.

In an article published soon after Miss X's evidence was taken, Ben Macintyre wrote, in the *Times Online,* that 'the term "God's access" has never before been deployed in public. Before this week, it did not even exist on the internet. But it is most certainly part of the lexicon now'.

Like all self-contained groups, be they professional or social, the intelligence community has its own lexicon. Such patois exists in order to keep outsiders out, and the initiated in, whether they be shared by teenagers, bloggers, or, in this case, spies. The slang and jargon of MI6 and other intelligence agencies – so-called 'spook-speak' – run in parallel with the much more vital codes used in their work. Spy networks are populated with **sleepers** (agents who infiltrate a target country and then lie low for a while), **babysitters** (bodyguards), **cobblers** (who can forge passports, or **shoes**, and identities), and **cleanskins** (undercover operatives on whom no police or security service file exists). All of whom may make **dead-drops**, the clandestine exchange of intelligence, or undertake **wet jobs**, secret operations which may involve bloodshed, particularly assassinations.

Surprisingly perhaps, some spy vocabulary has been borrowed from literature, rather than the other way round. John le Carré's writing has apparently been particularly productive: the term **mole**, designating a spy who works within an enemy country and sends secret information back to theirs, was said by le Carré to have been a KGB word originally, but it is largely thanks to his work that we know it today. **The Circus** has meanwhile become a nickname for the British Secret Service: again, it was first used by le Carré in his fiction before moving out into the mainstream. **Lamplighters** (watchers) and **pavement artists** (those who shadow someone) are just two more of le Carré's coinages. As Ben Macintyre puts it in his *Times* article, 'The real language of espionage and the invented language of literary spying are now so entwined that they cannot be untangled.'

The language of spying is clearly a fertile world. When we get a glimpse of it, as with 'God's access', it is as intriguing as the secret world behind it.

googleability

the ease with which a name or subject can be found by the Google search engine.

'**H**ow **googleable** are you?' asks the lexicographer Kerry Maxwell in her discussion of the latest spin-off of the phenomenally successful (linguistically as well as commercially) search engine. For the businesses and bloggers hoping to make it online the answer is crucial: **googleability** is all.

The term **Google** entered the *Oxford English Dictionary* in 2006, having proved beyond all doubt that it was here to stay. The verb **google** has become a generic term for using any search engine, in the same way that trademarks such as 'hoover', 'bandaid', 'xerox', and 'sellotape' have also entered the language as generic terms for their lookalikes as well as the originals. Further spin-offs, either from the Google enterprise itself or from its users, have further consolidated its success: we have **googlers** (those who google), **Gizoogle** (a rappers' version of Google), **Googlewhacking** (the challenge of finding a word which yields only one Google hit), **googlet** (any company bought by Google), and **googlicious**. And now there is 'googleability', or – its opposite – **ungoogleability**.

Donna Steinbraker, writing in the *International Herald Tribune*, laments the fact that 'the Googly eye sees all' and the lack of anonymity it brings. Regretting the entrenchment of 'a kind of Ur-busybody', she ponders whether in the future parents will choose their children's names according to their level of googleability: an unusual name would render someone far easier to find than the more common Mary or John. Parents would need to decide whether googleability or anonymity was the preferred option.

Ironically, the journalist behind the *Tribune* story doesn't exist, at least not as Donna Steinbraker: the name is googleable for this one article alone. A deliberate anti-Google move in which the writer, whatever his or her name, quite definitely gets the last laugh.

Googlegänger

a person who shares your name and who comes up as a Google 'hit' when you search for yourself.

In late 2007, the term **Googlegänger** began to catch our online imagination in the same way as the verb 'to google' itself had done some five years earlier. We are, in fact, the Google Generation: defined not by our real-world achievements but by our level of **googleability** (see page 49).

When we run a search of our name on the Google search engine – when, in other words, we indulge in a bit of **egosurfing** – most of us will find a group of people who share our name but with whom we have otherwise very little in common. We may even find that our name belonged to a deceased person whose existence is forever kept alive thanks to the Web's large holding of historical records. These people are our Googlegängers – the virtual version of doppelgängers but with the crucial difference that the resemblance stops there. They are our digital multiple selves.

For some, their virtual namesake may be a benign alter ego with whom they may converse on *Facebook*. For others, their Googlegänger is a competitor who beats them to the top Google position – a lifelong irritant from a cyber rival.

However we feel about them, searching out people who share our name is fast becoming one of our most popular online pastimes. As for the term itself, the American Dialect Society voted it the Most Creative Word of 2007.

800lb gorilla

a powerful or influential factor in something that is impossible to ignore or to resist.

Business jargon does not always merit its reputation for cliché and blandness. Much of it is inventive, particularly when it delivers the unexpected. The **800lb gorilla** may have originated in the joke 'Where does an 800lb gorilla sit? Answer: anywhere it likes'. The image has been used more widely in the US, but has begun to make an impact in the British business world and to cross the boundary into the mainstream. Most recently, it has begun to be used in the sense of 'a problem that everyone knows is there but that no one wants to raise'.

The metaphor was picked up by the US Congressman Edward Markey, who introduced a bill to make the extradition of terrorists for suspected torture illegal in US law. 'Extraordinary rendition,' he said, 'is the 800lb gorilla in our foreign and military policy-making that nobody wants to talk about.'

Animal imagery in business English – or 'Offlish' as it has been dubbed – is nothing new. Among the idioms to have emerged in this decade are **prairie-dogging** (the act of looking over an office partition wall to see what colleagues are doing, much as the prairie dog keeps watch of its colony by peering out of its burrow), **passing the monkey**, which is passing on a problem to someone else, and an **ideas hamster** (someone who runs energetically on the 'inspiration treadmill').

If these terms have remained largely within the confines of the office, the '800lb gorilla' is firmly in the mould of three other images of recent years that are now widely used outside it. A **moose on the table**, a **gorilla on the porch**, and an **elephant in the room** all denote an uncomfortable truth that no one alludes to in the hope it will go away (which of course it never does). Both phrases were coined in America in the 1960s and recall the allusion of the 'emperor's new clothes', the title of the Danish fairy tale by Hans Christian Andersen in which everyone can see that the emperor is walking naked, but dare not say anything – so they pretend he is fully clothed.

The 'elephant in the room' is beginning to address other unspeakables. It has become a regular image in the discussion (or not) of alcoholism within a family. If the '800lb gorilla' is already a potent image in the political arena, it seems to share the potential of establishing itself in mainstream English.

HIP

an acronym for 'Home Information Pack'.

After some delays and much criticism, the home information pack was finally rolled out on 14 December 2007. From that moment, all homes put on the market, no matter what size or value, are required by law to carry a **HIP**, which brings together key information needed by the buyer at the very start of the sales process. That information includes an energy performance certificate, title, and other standard searches such as the provision of water and drainage to the property, and a general sales statement on such matters as freehold/leasehold status.

HIPs were due to be rolled out in June 2007. They were the subject of an initial two-month delay before being introduced in August to cover only those properties with more than four bedrooms. Three-bedroom homes were added in the September, before the packs became mandatory for all homes in December.

From the outset, the packs were received with some prickliness. Opponents claimed that they would distort the housing market, lead to a fall in the national number of starter homes made available for sale, and make it harder for young people to get onto the property ladder. The government faced pressure from the other side too: advocates claimed that the delays were a result of a failure of nerve and a bowing to media pressure.

At least the British press found some enjoyment from the proceedings. Headlines such as 'Pack to the Future' and 'HIP pain!' (*Daily Mirror* and *The Sun*) seemed not without a touch of glee. Even the *Daily Mail*'s sombre 'Countdown to chaos over the home seller packs nobody wants' sounded a touch triumphant. For everyone else, however, 'HIP' is likely to be a simple acronym that belies the complexity of its requirements.

homedebtor

a homeowner with a very large mortgage, particularly one
that they are unlikely to ever pay off.

In an April 2008 edition of the online magazine *Slate* and an article
headed 'Here Comes the Next Mortgage Crisis', Mark Gimein
outlined the continuing battle facing homeowners whose mortgage
repayments are crippling them. 'If,' he wrote, 'you are one of the
homedebtors . . . you might start thinking very seriously about
just how attached you are to the wisteria vine snaking over the
basketball hoop on your garage.'

The inevitable result of **affluenza*** perhaps?

See also JINGLE MAIL and NINJA LOAN.

---

* An extreme form of materialism in which consumers overwork and accumulate high levels
of debt to purchase more goods: see page 94.

IPOD

an acronym for 'insecure, pressured, overtaxed, and debt-ridden'.

For those who thought the iPod was the digital music player par excellence, and the icon of the 21st century, a report by the think tank Reform entitled 'The Class of 2007' might make them reconsider. It projected that today's young face a bleak financial future, hit by a combination of student debts, rising living costs, and exorbitant property prices. This, Reform concluded, is the new **IPOD** generation: insecure, pressured, overtaxed, and debt-ridden.

Reform had first coined the acronym 'IPOD' two years earlier. The repetition of the message brought it back into currency amidst a climate of increasing financial insecurity for older as well as younger generations.

The prospect of the average graduate's salary being halved once taxes and other compulsory payments had been deducted had many commentators finding in 'IPOD' a distillation of all that is socially wrong in modern Britain. Foremost among them, somewhat inevitably, were voices from the government's opposition. Vince Cable, the Treasury spokesman for the Liberal Democrats, declared that 'Gordon Brown's obsessive tinkering with the tax system and introduction of top-up fees mean that graduates on modest salaries now face an unacceptably high tax burden.'

In an age where press releases and social reports proliferate, Reform's message was perfectly pitched. Their inspired neologism, which turned an accepted and fashionable term into something startlingly different, ensured that the 'IPOD generation' made headlines across broadsheets and tabloids alike. Taking the hottest accessory to the bleakest burden in one linguistic step was guaranteed to cause a stir.

IPOD

The nineties and noughties have seen a host of acronyms emerge to define certain social groups. It all began with the **Yuppies** (young, urban professionals) in the eighties, a term that has shown remarkable staying power and which, for those who witnessed the phenomenon, still requires no explanation at all. Whether the following will enjoy the same longevity is debatable, but they are nonetheless linguistic thumbprints of the society that produced the words and the people they described:

FIDs

Five years ago, Mark Honigsbaum described in *The Observer* the extension of the 'new man': the new father who spends quality time with his children, and whose input was said to be driving down juvenile crime and pushing up levels of literacy. Led by dads such as David Beckham, the fully involved dad (FID for short) 'juggles a double buggy in one hand and his children's lunchboxes and reading books just as adroitly in the other'. The opposite, of course, was the **FUD**, the fully uninvolved dad.

YADs

Today's young are not all marked down as ASBO-deserving troublemakers. 'Young and determined savers' are those fighting the odds of becoming an 'IPOD'. The term was coined by a National Savings and Investments Survey in 2004.

Skiers

If 'boomerang kids', who return home when they can't afford to live elsewhere, become **kippers** ('kids in parents' pockets eroding their savings'), 'skiers' are those who are bucking the trend and 'spending their kids' inheritance' on travel, health, and leisure pursuits. They are alternatively known as **woofs** ('well-off older folk').

Neets

According to the Office of National Statistics there are 1.2 million 16–24-year-olds in the UK who are 'not in education, employment, or training'. A recent study found that one in ten male Neets have been involved in crime, whilst female Neets are six times more likely to have a child by the age of 21.

ish

a slang term often used to replace or avoid the word 'shit'.

The editing of rap songs is a tricky business. Some would say that the whole point of that musical genre is to overstep the normal limits, including the boundaries of linguistic acceptability. On the other hand, a song needs to be heard if it is to succeed, and rap is no different. And for radio purposes, it needs to be cleaned up. The conversion of 'shit' to **ish** does exactly that.

For centuries, slang has served as a code among communities as diverse as teenagers and criminals. It is a shared language expressly designed to keep outsiders out, and insiders in: a badge of identity among peers. As a result, it needs to move quickly: as soon as parents or others have cracked the code it needs to be reinvented.

So it is that 'ish' came into being. Like **shizzle** in the early noughties – used as a euphemistic replacement for almost any word that required it, and famously in the phrase 'shizzle ma nizzle' – it was designed to be a word understood by its community but not to be understood by those outside it. It delivered its message while sidestepping those who would otherwise have disapproved. Either that, or 'ish' was something that nobody minded, giving the unpalatable what Quentin Crisp called, in his definition of a euphemism, the odour of 'diplomatic cologne'.

jingle mail

the practice of sending back one's house keys to the mortgage company because of negative equity, or the inability to keep up with payments.

In an article in *The New York Times* entitled 'Cruel Jokes, and No One Is Laughing', published in January 2008 when the repercussions from the US's 'subprime' (see below) fallout were daily news, Gretchen Morgenson reported on an increase in the number of people who were simply walking away from their homes because of their inability to keep up with mortgage payments. In doing so, some of these debtors were simply posting the house keys to their creditors, hence the punning term **jingle mail** as a representation of the tinkling packages of keys. Morgenson commented: 'There's nothing like black humor to define – however sadly and starkly – the blows that keep on coming in this mortgage debacle. But make no mistake, lenders are only beginning to learn how to manage the onslaught of jingle mail and houses turned inside out.'

Newspapers like *The New York Times* and the blogosphere were full of stories of clients who had lost hundreds of thousands of dollars as a result of the **credit crunch** and a fall in value of the house market of over 25%. They are the new **homedebtors**, owing on houses that have sunk **underwater** – fallen into negative equity. As one columnist in the *East Valley Tribune* of Arizona put it about one abandoned property: 'Most likely the house has gone "underwater" and the owners swam away.'

But not, presumably, before posting their jingle mail.

Subprime was undoubtedly one of the most prominent words of 2007, and one which has only increased in frequency as the meltdown of the US housing market continues. The term, used for mortgage packages taken out by those who cannot qualify for competitive rates because of a poor credit history and which carry higher interest rates and fees in order to compensate for the increased risk, was rapidly taken up by the British media and assimilated into our day-to-day vocabulary. It moved from the professional financial lexicon to the mainstream at blistering speed. Subprime was the villain in the piece that was the credit crunch.

Alongside this in the topical financial lexicon were other words which had crossed over from the specialist to the general. **Alt-A**, short for alternative A, was picked up to describe products that fall between traditional competitive mortgages and the subprime market: in other words, they carry rates and fees that are higher than standard mortgages but lower than subprime packages. An **exploding ARM**, meanwhile, describes a variable rate mortgage with rates that soon rise beyond a borrower's ability to pay.

Many of the terms used and readily understood today have shown remarkable longevity. In May 2008 *The Independent* reported on fears that Britain could once again be haunted by the spectre of **stagflation**. This portmanteau word, a blend of 'stagnation' and 'inflation', denotes a combination in an economic climate of stagnant growth and rising inflation. It was seen as the curse of the 1970s when Britain, together with many western countries, fell into recession. *The Telegraph* reported that the fear of stagflation's return contradicted any hopes that Britain had 'reached the bottom of the **bear** market' and was 'laying the foundation for a new **bull** market advance', employing two very old financial terms for economic health or the lack of it. A 'bear' is someone who sells shares in the expectation that they are about to fall in value – a pessimist, in other words. A 'bull', meanwhile, buys shares in the hope of selling them later at a higher price – an optimist. There are many colourful theories about the origin of both.

We do know that 'bear' and 'bull' have long histories. Both terms have been around since the beginning of the 18th century. 'Bear', firstly, is a contraction of the term 'bearskin jobber', who traded shares in the London Stock Exchange. There was a French proverb at the time which warned against over-optimism: 'Ne vendez pas la peau de l'ours avant de l'avoir tué' (Don't sell the bearskin before you've killed the bear). A bearskin jobber sold shares he didn't own in the hope of making the price fall, and then 'caught the bear' by buying them more cheaply just before he had to deliver.

A 'bull', meanwhile, may well have been coined as an alliterative analogy to 'bear'. A bull also drives ahead with full power and confidence, hence the adjective 'bullish' today.

'Subprime', 'jingle mail', 'Alt-A': the world's financial markets have been one of the biggest generators of vocabulary in 2007–8. New terms have emerged, and older ones have been resurrected: either way, specialized vocabulary is now firmly on the British public's radar. How low the economic downturn will take us is hard to predict, but as fears of a recession escalate, it may be productivity of the linguistic kind that is the safest bet.

junk sleep

low-quality sleep due to disturbances from nearby electronic devices such as mobile phones, laptop computers, and TVs.

First we have an epidemic of obesity from junk food. Now we have the sleep equivalent. Today's teenagers sleep next to so many distracting devices that their health is at risk from an epidemic of sleep deprivation.

Whether it is a mobile phone tucked under their pillow, the sound of music, the TV in the background – complete with the glowing lights of the stereo or screen – or a computer game that tempts them to play into the small hours of the morning, **junk sleep** has been deemed a major problem for teenagers worldwide. According to a recent survey, one in three schoolchildren is going to school on as little as four hours' sleep a night.

Clearly we need to watch our **sleep hygiene**: a term coined as far back as the 1890s to describe the principles ensuring a good night's sleep. Otherwise we will all succumb to **semisomnia**, another term that flourished in 2008 as a descriptor of a mild but chronic condition caused by poor sleep habits.

The sleep lexicon, rather like our days, is clearly not finished yet.

kinnear

to surreptitiously take a photograph of someone.

The precise origins of mint-new words, which make up only 1% of all new vocabulary, are notoriously difficult to track down. Not so with **kinnear**, which was invented on her personal blog by Stephanie Pearl-McPhee, who tried and failed to photograph the actor Greg Kinnear unawares when she spotted him at an airport. The resultant shots show only the lower legs of several passengers which really could have belonged to anyone.

The chances of survival for any new word are slim. Most are born in obscurity and the exact circumstances unknown. While 'kinnear' has the advantage over these, deliberate coinages are often especially doomed given the highly individual contexts which catalysed them. It will require considerable publicity and usage to stay alive. Certainly bloggers are taking it up – a positive sign when today the repetition of a word in online communities can make all the difference between success and failure. In the game of linguistic innovation, 'kinnear' certainly stands a fighting chance.

'Anyway, I Kinneared him. I forgot to take off the "ka-chinka" noise the camera-phone makes and made the hasty decision to lie still like I was some dead woodland creature if the noise alerted him to my activities. I hear it works for bears.'
(A knitting community blogger who had been stuck in the lift for an hour with a stranger, April 2008.)

Language, unlike photographs or publicity, is an area which no celebrity, however influential, can dictate. Whilst the evolution of a name into a linguistic shorthand for a particular attribute or style is one of the greatest displays of public recognition, the equations made may not always be complimentary. Nevertheless, if all publicity is good publicity, then a personal place in language may be highly sought-after. To have your name make it into a dictionary and become official, as Delia Smith did in 2001 when **doing a Delia** made it into the *Collins English Dictionary*, must count as one of the highest linguistic accolades.

Among those figures in recent times to have gained currency in the language are the Chelsea football captain John Terry, whose unfortunate missed penalty in the UEFA Champions League Final resulted in the rather inevitable verb **to terry**: to slip and miskick. Meanwhile, Quentin Tarantino still stands as a descriptor of an ominous, potentially violent situation: as in 'It's feeling a bit **Tarantino** around here'. Tony Blair was, in his time, heavily name-dropped in the figurative sense: **to be Blaired** could mean anything from being won over to New Labour's Cool Britannia to being trumped by an arch-rival, as Gordon Brown was widely supposed to have been.

Thanks to these, there has this century become a distinct possibility that the real cry of the would-be famous may become 'I'm a Celebrity. Get me In the Dictionary'. A (spoof) summary in the *New Statesman* by the comedian Julian Clary demonstrates the rich possibilities of the latest celebrity shorthand.

'I went to the Golden Joystick Awards but it turned out to be about computer games. How Rupert Everett is that? I had too many Charles Kennedys and found myself in a Naomi Campbell situation with a right Dale Winton [. . .] Suspect that my career has a touch of the Michael Barrymores. Feel like doing a John Stonehouse. To stop myself sliding into the full Gazza, I popped a couple of Judy Garlands and soon felt pretty Fern Britton.'

knork

an all-in-one eating tool that combines the prongs of a fork
with a sharp edge for cutting (blend of 'knife' + 'fork').

In late 2007 the supermarket chain Sainsbury's announced the
result of a survey into British eating habits. Our modern lifestyle,
apparently, is now so busy that the traditional family meal at the table
is all but extinct. Not only that, but because most meals are being
consumed on a sofa as a TV meal, our traditional cutlery is no longer
cutting the mustard. We are using a fork to do everything on a plate,
even if cutting power is clearly lacking. Enter the **knork**.

This clumsy coinage, a blend of 'knife' and 'fork', seems an
unlikely candidate for the dictionary. And yet it is not new. The
real knork was invented in 2003 by an American entrepreneur called
Mike Miller. The official company website tells us that the knork
incorporates 'critical modifications to the ages-old fork design',
enabling the user 'to both cut and spear food with only one utensil –
and one hand'.

In the wake of the renewed public interest in the knork, the etymological
detective Michael Quinion tells us that the cutlery lexicon is already a
crowded one. Decades ago, and again in the US, the **spork** was created:
a spoon with prongs. Although first recorded in the 1920s the 'spork'
was not trademarked until 1969: if it took a long time to make its mark,
however, the utensil (unlike its name, which sits alongside another
portmanteau word, the **foon**) is now in widespread use.

Australians have their own fork and spoon combination, known as a
spayd, a blend of 'spoon' and 'blayd'. The design was popularized in the
1960s and spayds are apparently (perhaps the British equivalent of fondue
sets) a standard, if much-mocked, wedding present.

Michael Quinion also reminds us of Edward Lear's **runcible spoon**, an idiosyncratic coinage by the humorist for his wonderful poem 'The Owl and the Pussy Cat'. Lear's own illustrations of it suggest it is simply a long-handled spoon, but the word has been applied by others to various designs, including one from the 1920s, and detailed in the *Oxford English Dictionary* as 'a kind of fork used for pickles, etc., curved like a spoon and having three broad prongs of which one has a sharp edge'.

Finally, there is the **Nelson fork**, used by Lord Nelson after the loss of his right arm in Tenerife in 1797. It has a single blade attached by a screw to the three fork tines. Passed on by Captain Hardy, it can be seen in the National Maritime Museum in Greenwich, while a gold version is kept by Lloyd's of London for special occasions.

latte liberal

someone who espouses the ideals of socialism whilst leading a less than egalitarian lifestyle.

The political lexicon is never richer than during a time of electoral campaigning. This goes particularly for name-calling. The race for the Democratic nomination between Barack Obama and Hillary Clinton, even if its ending saw them stand side by side, proved the point: the exchange of insults was at times as fast and furious as in any battle of left and right.

Barack Obama was called a **latte liberal** because of his perceived attempts to charm the coffee-drinking, left-leaning liberals. This was as opposed to his rival Senator Clinton, who seemed to have the white-collar workers firmly on her side. The insult came after one union leader called Obama supporters 'latte-drinking, Prius-driving, Birkenstock-wearing, trust-fund babies'.

Obama also attracted the term **Dunkin' Donut Democrat**, a **wine-track** politician compared with the **beer-track** Clinton.

Such epithets were hotly disputed by Obama's campaign camp, and the results of the race indeed suggested that a good proportion of non latte-drinking, non-wealthy Americans found in his favour. Nonetheless, as one columnist put it, 'the meme is out there, and it's sticking'.

In Britain, the 'latte liberal' tag carried clear echoes of the **champagne socialists** who claim to subscribe to socialist ideals while having an expensive tipple as they ponder them. Also known as **Bollinger Bolsheviks**, they are very much the equivalent of those targeted in the anti-Obama label.

69

Nor are such names limited to either side of the Atlantic. In Australia, such confused politicians are known as **chardonnay socialists**, in Ireland, as **smoked salmon socialists**, in Poland, the **caviar left** ('kawiorowa lewica'), in Sweden, the **red wine leftists** ('rödvinsvänster'), and in Chile, the **whisky socialists**. In 1992, Labour leader John Smith's mission to charm workers in the City of London over lunch became known as the **prawn cocktail offensive**, prompting the then Deputy Prime Minister Michael Heseltine to quip: 'Never have so many crustaceans died in vain.' (The culmination of the metaphorical feast was the clarion cry 'Save the prawns!')

Clearly **kitchen-table politics**, made up of **bread and butter issues**, have had something of a gastronomic upgrade. But then that's probably the point.

lifestream (verb)

to make a continuous digital record of one's life in video, sound, images, and print.

First there was the **blog**, a hugely successful phenomenon which has been to the 21st century what diaries were to the 18th. In 2008 we have taken several virtual steps further. The new online black is the creation of a detailed online record of one's life: a **lifestream**.

Lifestreamers collect data about their daily lives and create an online record of their activities, drawing together content posted across the Web, whether on a blog, on a social networking site such as *Facebook* and *MySpace*, or on other online media such as *YouTube* or audio podcasts. The result is a three-dimensional online identity and a virtual home that friends can visit and add to. A streamer's life is simulcast 24 hours a day.

That anyone would want to do this has been the source of bemusement for some. Writing in the *Sunday Tribune*, Damien Mulley (in an article entitled 'Being Damien Mulleyvitch') despairs of the prospect of a Web which operates as a 'digital smorgasbord':

'Now users can display their posts from their blog, they can display the drunken pics that they uploaded to Flickr, show the embarrassing videos they have from their YouTube profile and so much more. . . . This is the idea behind 'lifestreaming' and is a dream come true for those that gloriously show off every facet of their life and the millions of lurkers who are willing to tune into such dross.'

The creation of an online identity has been one of the most prominent themes of the 21st century thus far. Social networking is no longer situated in physical space; it is now all about setting yourself up in the

71

virtual world and sharing details of your life via photographs, video, music, and messages.

If 'lifestreaming' is the word of the moment, it had a worthy predecessor in the very thing it has extended, the **blog**, which is one of the most prominent neologisms to be created this century and one that is still going strong. Such is the success of the phenomenon (which has surely been influenced by the equal popularity of the word) that few of us today would be unaware of its meaning. Coined in the closing years of the 20th century, the growing number of linguistic spin-offs are ample demonstration that 'blog', a blend of 'web' and 'log', is a survivor. From the original term have sprung **moblog** and **phlog** (sharing photos, often from mobile phones), **vlog** (video blogging), **splog** (a spam-like technique for exploiting inter-blog references), **plog** (a political blog), and **flog** (which can be glossed in multiple ways, including a 'fake blog').

Lifestreaming is also generating its own vocabulary: lifestreamers' office counterparts are the **workstreamers**, who create a daily account of their working lives for the benefit of colleagues and even employers. **Lifecasting** is the continual digital broadcasting of one's lifestream via a portable camera which streams first-person video footage: otherwise known as a **lifeblog**, **lifeglob**, **cyborglog**, or **glog**.

limbo skating

the sport and hobby of skateboarding under cars and other obstacles.

Also known as **roller-limbo**, the combination of the limbo position and skating at high-speed has proved irresistible in places as far afield as Udaipur in India and Beijing. Its arrival in the UK is hotly anticipated, more so since *The Guardian* published an article about the exploits of Aniket Chindak, who is hoping to seize the title of world **limbo-skating** champion by skating under 100 parked cars:

'Last March, he successfully skated under 57 cars in 45 seconds. He began skating at the age of 18 months, and it took three months of practice to achieve the right position for limbo-skating. . . . Last September, three-year-old Krishna Kunwar Gahlo of Udaipur skated under a bus with a clearance height of 11in, and in October, five-year-old Uttam Gahlot, also from Udaipur, rolled under a car with a clearance height of just 6.75in, which his coach claimed to be a record in the boys' category.' (*The Guardian*, 3 January 2008.)

The title 'Roller Limbo Princess' of America, meanwhile, belongs to 7-year-old Zoey Beda from Wisconsin. Footage of her astonishing feats can be seen on *YouTube*. A report from the Associated Press is commentary enough: 'With Chubby Checker's "Limbo Rock" pumping from the speakers, she gets within a few feet of the bar, drops into the full splits, hands grabbing her ankles, dips her head under the bar and rolls under, her pigtails grazing the floor.'

The lowdown in every sense.

locavore

a consumer who buys only locally-produced food and other goods.

Personal preferences have always dictated our dietary habits. Whether we be vegetarians or carnivores, our food choices have become as much a statement about ourselves as our taste in clothes or music.

Now, however, the debate has widened, and climate change is affecting our food choices too. The availability of foods from right across the globe has meant an explosion of different cuisines on our supermarket shelves, whether it be grapes from Chile or coffee from Guatemala. Ironically, this opening up of our culinary horizons has seen those of our planet shrinking: transporting our food thousands of miles to our plate is a luxury we are beginning to realize we can no longer afford. Airmiles, at least when buying food, have a whole new meaning.

Enter the **locavores**, environmentally-aware consumers who will put only locally-produced food on their plates.

The locavores were originally a group of friends in California. They gave each other the singular challenge of eating only what they could find within a 100-mile radius of their homes. The name was the invention of four women in San Francisco, a self-described 'group of concerned culinary adventurers', to coincide with World Environment Day in 2005. The followers of the local foods movement had a new name, and a new momentum.

The lexicon of dietary disciplines and their followers is a growing one. There are **vegans**, **fruitarians**, **lactarians**, **opportunivores**, and **freegans**, all characterized by their dietary and moral principles (proponents of the latter two categories eat only what is free, whether found in the wild, including roadkill, or thrown out by others as waste). Now, to be a locavore is to make a statement about our environmental concerns and our ever-increasing awareness of our global 'footprint'.

If more and more people subscribe to what has been alternatively termed **food patriotism**, the resources of our world will almost certainly be richer. Ironically, however, our language will be poorer: English has long been a master at importing foreign words from all corners of the globe. A large proportion of imports in recent decades has been the result of an explosion of interest in foreign cuisine. Should that interest be stemmed, so will the tide of new culinary vocabulary.

That, though, is surely a small price to pay: language is robust; our planet may not be.

See also ETHICUREAN.

McQualification

a term coined by the British press to denote skills qualifications issued by companies such as McDonald's.

On 28 January 2008, Gordon Brown and his new Work and Pensions Secretary, James Purnell, signalled an acceleration of welfare reform by pledging to withhold benefits from anyone refusing work-training, and backing a new initiative to allow private companies to confer qualifications and rewards upon in-house employees.

On the same day, McDonald's announced the 'important and exciting step' of being one of the first firms to offer its own nationally recognized qualifications from courses approved by the Qualifications and Curriculum Authority.

Somewhat predictably, the media had a field day. The move came not long after considerable attention had been given to a campaign by McDonald's to ban the word 'McJob' (defined as an unstimulating, low-paid job with few prospects) from the *Oxford English Dictionary*. Headlines such as 'Would you like a **McQualification** with your **McJob**?' appeared in countless blogs within minutes of the government's intentions going public. By the following morning, it was mentioned in almost every national newspaper, tabloid and broadsheet alike. And the wordplay didn't stop there: the *Financial Times* decided upon **McA-level**, the *Education Guardian* the **McNVQ**, and other pods and blogs the **McCheeseCSE**. The Mcformula, it seemed, is just too tempting to resist.

manscaping

the all-over removal of a man's body hair as part of a grooming routine (blend of 'man' + 'landscaping').

Below the sensational(-ist) headline '**Manscaping** Takes Manhattan! Dudes Denude Their Woolly Nether Parts', the tell-it-like-it-is *New York Observer* described the latest in cosmetic procedures for men: manscaping, which 'is transforming the bodies of an unlikely segment of the population . . . Manhattan's overachieving heterosexual business *machers*, Wall Street dudes'. (A macher, incidentally, is a 'big shot'.)

The surge in grooming procedures for men is well documented. 'Manscaping' is the linguistic successor to the 'back, sack, and crack' shave and physically goes one step further. For this is the removal of hair from *all* parts of the male body, and not just the nether regions. According to the men's magazine *Maxim*, 'having too much body hair is akin to having too little head hair'.

However seductive the latest fashion might be, not everyone is convinced. *USA Today* explained in its discussion of a term which is just beginning to make headway over here:

'Even cowboys get the back-hair blues. At Napoleon's for Men, a 2-year-old hot-shave-and-haircut hangout in Boise, guys who are no strangers to reins and rifles will occasionally call and ask whether waxing hurts. "I say, 'You can handle it,'" receptionist Dayna Ross says.'

It might be worth asking them again afterwards.

See also BOYTOX.

misspeak

(mainly US) to express oneself in an insufficiently clear or accurate way.

In the course of her presidential nomination campaign, Senator Hillary Clinton set out her stall as the candidate with first-hand experience of a military front line by recounting her dramatic arrival in Bosnia's airport during her time as First Lady. She related the drama of sniper fire that forced her and colleagues to run 'with our heads down to get into the vehicles to get to our base'. A few weeks later footage was broadcast by CBS News that suggested a rather different introduction to the war zone. Viewers saw the First Lady waving to well-wishers as she descended from her plane, and the subsequent greeting given to her by a young girl who recited a poem.

The discrepancy between Clinton's own portrayal of the events of that day and the facts as shown in the documentary evidence fuelled accusations by rivals that this was just one more example of a persistent pattern of exaggeration. It went along, in their view, with the Senator's claims that she was party to many powerful decisions during her time as First Lady in the White House, including a hand in brokering peace in Northern Ireland. Clinton described her previous statement as a rare error: 'This has been a very long campaign . . . Last week for the first time in 12 years or so, I **misspoke**.'

'**M**isspoke' appeared to be a careful and deliberate choice of words. In almost all transcripts of her remarks the word was rendered in quotation marks, including this from *The Independent*:

'It was during an editorial board interview with the Philadelphia Daily News, published yesterday, that Mrs Clinton was finally forced to confess she "misspoke" about the Tuzla trip. "I think that, a minor blip, you know, if I said something that, you know, I say a lot of things – millions of words a day – so if I misspoke it was just a misstatement," she said.'

A spokesman for Clinton's rival, Barack Obama, noting that the Senator made her claims in a scripted speech, also picked up on her careful wording. 'When you make a false claim that's in your prepared remarks, it's not misspeaking, it's misleading.'

While 'misspeak' means simply making an inaccurate statement, it most often allows the withdrawal of a statement without the making of a damaging admission. In other words: a transparent euphemism. As such it is regularly the subject of parody when it comes to political-speak. The US presidential drama *The West Wing* has used it on more than one occasion to signal political obfuscation. In one episode, a spokeswoman's error in describing the President's attitude to an urgent political issue is lamented by her colleagues, Leo McGarry, Josh Lyman, and Toby Ziegler:

Leo: What did she say?
Josh: She said the President's relieved to be focussing on something that matters.
Leo: *Relieved?*
(Leo turns, fuming and shaking his head.)
[. . . .]
Toby: She misspoke is all we need. We go back, we say she misspoke.

The implication behind the quotation marks used in the reporting of Senator Clinton's retraction clearly served to cast doubt over her veracity. That she employed a term that is regularly used as a clear-cut euphemism was deemed by many to be unfortunate. It was probably inevitable that it provoked comparisons with another choice of phrase, also apparently chosen with great care, this time used by her husband Bill Clinton during his impeachment over the Monica Lewinsky affair. The President's denial, which was legalistically highly careful, prompted equal speculation as to the truth of the matter. As a result it quickly became shorthand for the entire proceedings: 'It depends on what the meaning of the word "is" is.'

Senator Clinton's attempt to retrieve an error rather than to acknowledge it has many precedents, among them the then Cabinet Secretary Sir Robert Armstrong, who quoted, during the Spycatcher trial in 1986, the orator and political theorist Edmund Burke in the following exchange:

Lawyer: What is the difference between a misleading impression and a lie?
Armstrong: A lie is a straight untruth.
Lawyer: What is a misleading impression – a sort of bent untruth?
Armstrong: As one person said, it is perhaps being 'economical with the truth'.

'Misspeak' also has echoes of the White House Secretary Ronald Ziegler's comment about all of Richard Nixon's previous comments on Watergate, namely that 'all previous statements are inoperative'.

momnesia

a pattern of mental confusion and forgetfulness that characterizes a mother's first year after giving birth.

The term **momnesia**, a blend of 'mom' and 'amnesia', was coined by neurologists in 2008 after research confirmed that there is a biological basis for memory lapses. Their findings suggested that such mental fuzziness may actually represent an evolutionary advantage by blocking out all extraneous matters and allowing a mother to concentrate entirely on nurturing her newborn. The neuroscientist Louann Brizendine, author of *The Female Brain*, believes that 'other parts of your brain that are usually on high alert are sort of taken offline [. . .] You're on the mother beat all the time. It requires certain parts of your brain to work hyper, hyper, hyper well. But it requires other parts of your brain to play second fiddle.'

Scientists believe that hormones may also play a part in 'momnesia', notably oestrogen levels which are extremely high in late pregnancy but which plummet dramatically after delivery. As oestrogen acts as a neurotransmitter, sending signals to the brain, such a significant drop in its levels may impair mental acuity.

As if we needed science to prove it.

'Blending', the linguistic process whereby two or more words are fused to become one, is a productive generator of new words. It is estimated that over 5% of all neologisms result from such combinations.

Many blends are tongue-in-cheek, and as such tend to have a shorter lifespan than other new words. They nonetheless account for some of the most inventive vocabulary to be coined each year, and are also the fastest to spread. Among blends of recent years are **cankle**, a thick ankle ('calf' + 83 'ankle'), **blipvert** (= 'blip' + 'advert': a very short commercial), **webisode** (= 'web' + 'episode), **waparazzi** ('WAP', for Wireless Application Protocol, the technology behind the latest mobile phones, + 'paparazzi'), and, of course, the highly successful **blog**, an online journal ('web' + 'log'), and **podcast** ('iPod' + 'broadcast'), denoting digital audio content which is downloadable to an MP3 player.

'Momnesia' caught the attention of the English-speaking media in a way that a more sober scientific label would not have done. In its cheeriness it also avoided the pitfall of patronizing mothers who have long recognized their reduced ability to concentrate in the early months of child-rearing. Thanks to such qualities it is likely to show greater longevity than other blends that arise more from our love of wordplay than to fulfil any pressing linguistic need.

moofer

an acronym for a mobile out-of-office worker.

A **moofer** is one of the new generation of office workers who are given the flexibility to choose where, when, and how they want to work according to the task in hand.

M **oofing** was coined by a Microsoft worker, James McCarthy, in his blog entitled *Mr Moof*. He describes moofers, and those who have the courage to employ them, as 'people who understand that work is something you do, not somewhere you go'. He criticizes the traditional policy among companies of 'presenteeism, where workers are measured on input, i.e. hours worked, rather than the output of their endeavours'. It probably won't be long before he also speaks of 'moofers and shakers'.

mosquito

an electronic device which emits an unpleasant high-frequency sound, similar to the buzz of a mosquito, and which is audible primarily to younger people. It is intended as a deterrent to youths who loiter in certain locations and whose presence is intimidating to shopkeepers and members of the public.

The **mosquito** was developed by a security consultant Howard Stapleton as an anti-nuisance device. Its high-pitched sound waves can be heard for the most part by children and young adults only, whose ability to hear high-frequency sound has not yet deteriorated with age. When the mosquito is switched on, it emits a highly annoying, insect-like buzzing sound.

Many shopkeepers who have installed the device have reported a reduction in antisocial behaviour by youths in the vicinity of their shop. However, there has been considerable opposition to the mosquito from human rights groups, and in 2008 a campaign was launched to ban the device, neatly called 'Buzz Off'. Other groups protest that the noise contravenes environmental laws; at present, however, the UK government has made no plans to enforce its withdrawal from the market.

Whether or not this new take on the name of the mosquito will earn a place in the dictionary will depend on its fortunes in the marketplace and its long-term legal status. It is an interesting turn of fate, however, that the unique advantage of the product, namely that it can be heard only by the young, has been exploited by the very group it is intended to deter. Teenagers have begun to choose the buzz as a ringtone which their friends can hear but which adults cannot. With this new high-frequency ring tone, students reportedly can receive text-message alerts on their cell phones without the teacher knowing. The audio equivalent of slang, perhaps?

mullet strategy

a strategy applied to the design of a website, whereby the initial interface is professional and slick, but the content behind it is user-generated and often far less impressive.

The term 'mullet hairstyle', a cut that is short in the front but long at the back, first appeared in written form in a 1994 song by the Beastie Boys, entitled 'Mullet Head'. It was later popularized by the country singer Billy Ray Cyrus with his track 'I want my mullet back'. It is a curious source of inspiration for a business term, but that is exactly what lies behind the new term **mullet strategy**, a concept that gives a website a 'sharp' upfront but a slightly less tidy back-end. The principle, in other words, is to increase traffic to the site by an eye-catching front page, while letting users generate the content.

The term was coined by Jonah Peretti, one of the founders of the *Huffington Post* Internet newspaper. Peretti has explained that the mullet approach means clean and shiny welcome pages while 'the shaggy, unedited user-generated content is stuffed into a closet several clicks away, not visible from the front hall' (*The Boston Globe*, 6 April 2008). It is 'business up front, party in the back'.

The term has proved catchy. It was quickly picked up by online lexicons and by bloggers who were soon playing around with derivatives such as **mulletocracy**. As Jan Freeman in her *Boston Globe* article says, 'everyone has an opinion on the mullet, if not the mullet strategy'.

nanofood

food which is produced by means of 'nanotechnology'.

Nanotechnology is a relatively new area of science in which matter is studied and controlled on an ultra-small scale: one nanometre is one millionth of a millimetre. Nanotechnology has made it possible to manipulate atoms and molecules in materials used in many different fields, including medicine, engineering, and, now, the food industry.

Nanofood is the result of the use of nanotechnological science in any part of the food chain, be it cultivation, production, or packaging. Some of the techniques being trialled include intelligent packaging with sensors which can detect the gases given off by the deterioration of food, and 'smart dust' which will transmit information to a farmer about the state of his crops or his livestock.

Nanotechnology has been the source of controversy right from the start as a result of its potential far-reaching applications right across our society. Opponents believe that human health and our environment may well suffer if nanoscience develops unchecked.

In 2004, the Prince of Wales called upon the Royal Society to review urgently the possible implications of nanotechnology and the possibility that reality may not follow the 'rose-tinted script'. The result was much gleeful reporting by the media that the Prince was issuing doom-laden warnings of **grey goo**, a term coined by the molecular nanotechnology pioneer Eric Drexler and subsequently picked up by science-fiction writers and the popular press as the prospect of an end-of-world scenario in which self-replicating robots consume all living matter on the planet. The Royal Society subsequently concluded in a report that such an outcome was not possible.

It was fairly inevitable therefore that the prospect of 'nanofood' alarmed many, just as the prospect of **genetically modified** or **GM** food did a decade earlier. Indeed like 'GM', 'nanofood' has already taken on the nickname **Frankenfood**, denoting something freakish, ugly, or unnatural as critics reached back to the 1800s and Mary Shelley's novel for what they saw as just the right allusion.

In May 2008 experiments on mice suggested that nano carbon tubes, used in a whole variety of everyday goods such as tennis rackets and bicycle wheels to make them both light and very strong, can cause serious lung disease. Nanotechnology looks to have some way to go to appease its critics.

Nerdic

a term created to describe computer- and technology-related English.

In the spring of 2008 the online electronics company Pixmania applied to the Foreign and Commonwealth Office to have a new language officially recognized, one spoken, they argued, by some 700 million people across the world (and so substantially more than Cornish, recently recognized and boasting around 2,000 speakers). This new language they termed **Nerdic**: the terminological and technological lexicon which is drawn upon across the board, 'from tech-toddlers to Wii-playing grannies' – in other words, geek-speak.

Pixmania's pitch to have Nerdic recognized was based on the company's assertion that the 'language' also has a unique pronunciation and grammar, as well as an independent vocabulary. It also crosses international boundaries, they maintain, with sentences such as 'an N96 with HSDPA, Wi-Fi with a 5 megapixel Carl Zeiss and GPS' being readily comprehensible across Europe, and the word 'Internet' being 3,000 times more popular in France than 'la toile d'araignée mondiale' in spite of the best efforts of the French Academy. From 'dongle' to 'Wi-Fi', Nerdic is growing at a faster rate than English proper.

To prove their point, Pixmania compiled a list of the top ten Nerdic phrases to look out for in 2008. Many will already be familiar to the technologically-minded. They include **RFID**, an abbreviation of radio-frequency identification which allows the tracking of goods around the world, **HDMI**, a new type of Scart lead that allows the connection of high-definition devices together, 'like your TV to your new Blu-ray player', and **fuel cell**, a green water-powered battery for everything from cars to laptops that will boost a gadget's life considerably over standard batteries.

They may not trip off the tongue – but then, for all its beauty, neither does Cornish.

NINJA loan

a loan or mortgage made to someone who has 'No Income, No Job, and No Assets'.

For many commentators witnessing the dramatic turndown in the fortunes of the US property market, the meltdown was both predictable and preventable. They point to the large number of 'subprime' high-risk loans made to unsuitable applicants without the appropriate checks into their circumstances. During a long period of steadily increasing house prices, some lenders were dispensing with details of their borrowers' background, requiring little or no information as to their ability to repay. 'One mortgage provider,' complained the *Institutional Investor* in 2007, 'advertises itself as the "home of the **'no-doc'** loan." Among the products listed on its website is the **NINJA loan**: Even borrowers with "No Income, No Job and No Assets" are welcome to apply.'

Ninja loans and their less colourfully named counterparts were one of the root causes of proliferating mortgage defaults, driving some of the subprime lenders into bankruptcy in the process.

In Japanese culture, a ninja was someone who was specially trained in the art of war, albeit of an unorthodox and clandestine kind. At the heart of their training were the tactics of espionage, the learning of martial arts, and methods of assassination: all equipping them for dangerous missions in the quest to defeat their feudal enemies.

The term 'ninja' became better known in the West during and after World War II when the warriors were the frequent subject of fiction. Most popularly, they featured in comic strips such as those created by Frank Miller in Marvel's *Daredevil* comics of the late 70s and early 80s, stories that were then satirized in the animated TV series *Teenage Mutant Ninja*

Turtles, a fictional team of four turtle mutants who are trained to become skilled ninja warriors and to fight evil from their sewers in Manhattan.

Clearly a high-risk loan has little in common with a crime-busting turtle. Where, however, 'ninja' scored was in its memorability: a link to popular culture such as this and attention is guaranteed, even for an acronym. Certainly for a company marketing a high-risk loan the resonances of successful warriors would not have been unwelcome.

'Ninja' sits alongside another sobriquet, harnessed by opponents of risky borrowing rather than its sellers: **liar loans** are self-certification mortgages – the borrower is trusted to state their income without needing to verify it.

There are many more words and phrases which were born out of cartoons. The **curate's egg** was first used in an 1895 *Punch* cartoon which featured a meek curate who, having been given a stale egg by his episcopal host, stated that 'parts of it' were 'excellent'. The **foo** in **foo-fighter**, used to describe unidentified lights encountered by airborne forces during the Second World War, and sometimes interpreted as enemy weapons, was a nonsense word which appeared in the 'Smoky Stover' comic strip by American cartoonist Bill Holman. A **goon** – a stolid, stupid, or dull person – came from the name of a subhuman creature called Alice the Goon in a popular US cartoon series by E. C. Segar, while a **hooligan** may derive from a comic Irish character of that name which appeared in a series of adventures in the London comic magazine *Funny Folks*. **Whammy** (now so often used in the term 'double whammy') was certainly popularized by, if not created for, the 'L'il Abner' comic strip of the 1950s.

nomophobia

a fear of being out of mobile phone contact. The word is a contraction of 'no mobile phone phobia'.

In the spring of 2008 a new affliction for the 21st century was announced. **Nomophobia** was coined to reflect the stress of being without a mobile phone or of being uncontactable by one in an area of poor reception. According to research conducted by the Post Office and made public in March, more than 13 million people admitted to experiencing feelings of anxiety when they run out of battery or credit, lose their phone or have no network coverage.

Nomophobia follows in the wake of other social 'diseases' that are regularly announced by researchers and PR companies. **Affluenza**, a portmanteau of 'influenza' and 'affluence', was a term coined in the opening years of the 21st century to describe the pursuit of wealth and material goods at any cost, including mounting debt.

Social groups are, it seems, a popular target for commercial neologizing, just as they are for governments which, after identifying them, then aim to target them. Among words coined by companies in this decade are **framily**, a term for friends to whom one becomes as close as to blood family members and who make up one's main support network, and **togethering**, the trend of travelling together with friends or colleagues for a holiday and some shared 'quality time' (a longer-lived, if now much-lampooned, term of the nineties).

Words such as these tend to be created primarily in order to be reported or reproduced with a commercial message. As such, they are less likely to survive than words that endure through a constant impetus of use and distribution. The case of 'nomophobia' may well prove an exception to the rule. It has already been heralded as a word that fills a distinct linguistic gap, and which needed to be invented. Losing your mobile is after all the greatest fear of those of us in today's **Generation D**: the generation that has grown up in the digital age.

non-dom

a person who is working in the UK but whose main interests are abroad. The term is short for 'non-domicile'.

According to the Treasury, there are around 116,000 foreigners who work in the UK and who have non-domicile status. In January 2008 the Chancellor Alistair Darling caused some consternation when he announced draft legislation to change the way these **non-doms** would be taxed. Until now, non-UK residents working here have paid tax only on their UK earnings. The proposed changes would mean that non-doms who have lived in the UK for more than seven years would be taxed on their worldwide earnings, rather than just those in this country, or have to pay an annual charge of £30,000.

The impact of such changes was illustrated by the US philanthropist Carol Colburn Hogel, who wrote in a letter to *The Scotsman*, 'I am heading back to North America, where an individual with involvement in, and charitable contributions to, visual arts and classical music is valued, not punished.'

Ms Hogel was not alone. When the legislation was confirmed in the Chancellor's first budget, many anticipated that hundreds of non-doms would move their financial affairs to Switzerland.

It was perhaps inevitable, then, that on many blogs and online comment sites was to be found the headline 'I'm a Non-Dom. Get Me Out of Here'.

nonebrity

a person who acquires and maintains celebrity status while having done little to deserve it.

In December 2007 the straight-talking *Sun* published its own guide to the movers and shakers in the language world: words which they had helped imprint on the British consciousness or which had simply taken their fancy. The headline to their piece was classic *Sun*-speak: 'A **nonebrity** with nice heavage'.

Leaving aside 'heavage' (the cult of very large breasts), 'nonebrity' is one of many words to have been coined by the spoof thesaurus *Roger's Profanisaurus*, authored by the creators of the comic *Viz*. It is defined as 'a pointless media figure who would love to rise up high enough to scrape on to the bottom end of the D-list'.

Unfortunately for those about to enter the Australian jungle, there were the inevitable 'I'm a Nonebrity . . .' type parodies. From the *Profanisaurus* to the outback may seem a very big step, but in the world of chat forums and tabloid newspapers, it took only a few virtual ones.

nubrella

a new kind of handle-less umbrella which requires no holding and which sits on the user's shoulders.

The **nubrella**, trademarked in 2008, is no ordinary rain-sparing device. A big plastic dome that sits on the shoulders and allows you to carry on using your hands for carrying, phoning, or texting, it looks, in the words of *ABC News*, 'like something out of a bad science fiction movie'. The protection from the weather, they continue, comes at a cost: 'Let's just call it the dorkiness factor.'

The inventor of the nubrella (the 'nu-umbrella'), Alan Kaufman, believes that the umbrella concept needs innovation, having not changed in 3,000 years. His invention is able to withstand winds of up to 50 mph, and keeps heat locked inside the dome.

Highly practical, according to those who have tried it, as long as you like the goldfish look. As one website flatly put it: 'Tomorrow's fashion mistake, today!' And yet, given the media attention the nubrella received on its launch, the definition of 'hands-free' may yet need a little refining.

olderpreneur

a middle-aged or older entrepreneur.

You no longer have to be young to be an entrepreneur: in 2008 the **olderpreneur** was born. As Britain's professional population ages, pension schemes deliver less than they promised, and new jobs become a statistical rarity over the age of 50, more and more men and women approaching retirement are increasingly taking matters into their own hands and starting up their own businesses. As Sir Alan Sugar, arguably Britain's most famous entrepreneur, has put it: 'Some people believe that when you get past a certain age of 50 that it's all over. Well, they're wrong, they're totally wrong.'

The term was apparently coined by a new website, *The Olderpreneur*, launched by the charity PRIME and aimed at providing people aged 50 and above with practical advice and news on business issues and enterprise. According to PRIME's marketing and research officer, 'the word olderpreneur and the website are part of our campaign to raise awareness about older entrepreneurs'. The charity aims to provide such people 'with a place to network, and overcome the issues and isolation they face'.

'Olderpreneur' follows on from various new groups identified and labelled in the 2000s, with the emphasis on a new lifestyle unhampered by the normal strictures of the workplace and its demands. Among them are **soul proprietors**: those who pursue an alternative, less work-driven lifestyle, one that enables spiritual growth with a positive **joy-to-stuff ratio** (the time available to an individual to enjoy life rather than that spent in working hard and collecting material goods – which there is of course increasingly less time to enjoy). In other words, the 'work/life balance' that has become such a stock phrase in recent years.

This desire on the part of some urban professionals to embrace a less stressful, simpler life, with greater spiritual or moral depth, has produced further words in the business lexicon. **Ecolonomics**, which focuses on environmentally sound business practices, is fast gathering proponents. Meanwhile the **alterpreneurs**, those who place more importance on their quality of life than profit-making, may welcome today's **experience economy**, in which we desire to do and feel rather than simply spend money.

The **mouse race** is the new lower-stress lifestyle, playing on 'rat race', which has been around since the 1950s to describe a relentless work ethic. This is **voluntary simplicity**: a lifestyle chosen so as to avoid **conspicuous consumption** and rather to embrace **conspicuous austerity**.

Such words speak to a new lifestyle, one which is carefully choreographed to reflect simple living, either by an absence of material goods or by the choice of obviously inferior ones. Of course, it doesn't always satisfy: an **upshifter** is someone who re-joins the high stress of professional life having experimented with **downshifting** and decided against it. The olderpreneurs of the future, perhaps?

peaknik

a person who believes that the global production of oil has peaked, or is about to, and that the results of such a peak will be economic and social collapse. The term is an adaptation of 'peacenik'.

Peak oil is the term used for the moment at which the maximum rate of oil production is reached. **Peakniks** are those who believe that, if global consumption is not reduced before that moment, an energy crisis will develop with catastrophic consequences for the human race. The concept of peak oil was first set out in 1956 by M. King Hubbert: the Hubbert Theory has been used to predict global oil-consumption rates and their likely peak.

The most pessimistic forecasts of a peak predict that it will take place very soon, if indeed it hasn't already. The more optimistic economists believe it will happen in ten to twenty years' time, and that we will have plenty of warning beforehand. Peakniks, who belong in the first category, fear a chain reaction from the oil peak which will initiate poverty on a large scale and the collapse of industrial civilization as we know it.

There is one category of peaknik who take their pessimism even further, and believe that, without oil, the earth will not have the natural resources to carry its population. The outcome would be famine and a collapse so catastrophic that human numbers may decline to the levels that existed before the Industrial Revolution. These peakniks are known as **doomers**, an abbreviation of 'gloom-and-doomer'.

There have been many words formulated on the '-nik' model, '-nik' being a suffix in Russian denoting a member of a class or group, or a supporter of a cause. It came into English largely via the

Russian earth satellite series **sputnik**, which in turn influenced the formation of the **beatniks** of the sixties Beat Generation. **Peacenik** came about in the 60s and 70s, when it was particularly used of opponents of US military intervention in Vietnam.

There are numerous 'peaknik' forums on the Web, while the term is also used of a whole category of economists and authors. Such exposure, and the liveliness of a debate that looks set to run and run, means that it is likely to stick around for some time to come.

PICNIC

an acronym for 'Problem In Chair Not In Computer'.

PICNIC is a term used by IT support personnel to describe someone who calls them to fix a problem with their hard- or software, when the problem is in fact due to their inexperience or incompetence.

Perhaps the computer was not switched on in the first place?

Acronyms in business are nothing new: indeed 'Offlish' is renowned for them. More often than not, they are seen as being just another example of impenetrable jargon.

Certainly, few would contest that business-speak can be infuriatingly opaque. Beyond such well-worn phrases as 'low-hanging fruit', 'pushing the envelope', 'blue-sky thinking', and 'core competencies' have come and gone an enervating line-up of euphemisms and clichés. And yet all communities have their own linguistic shorthand, and for good reason: both speed and understanding are served by a common language.

Arguably, acronyms serve such aims even better than idioms, which can sometimes be too clever and self-conscious to really aid plain-speaking. Technology-driven industries rely on acronyms and shortcuts more than any other: within the mobile-phone industry are thousands of abbreviations and acronyms which are readily understood by those in the know and, crucially, across national boundaries. **RFID** (radio frequency identification), **NFC** (near-field communication), **GSM** (the global system for mobile communications), and **VAD** (voice activity detection) are just four of those terms designed to aid quick communication.

Of course, there are many more acronyms which entertain along the way, of which PICNIC is certainly one. **UCWAP** (in trouble, or Up A Creek Without A Paddle), **WAMBAM** (Web Application Meets Bricks and Mortar), **WOMBAT** (Waste of Money, Brains, and Time), and **TA** (Thanks Again) get to the point quickly, if with a little cynicism thrown in.

podslurping

the theft of corporate data by installing special software on an iPod or similar device and then connecting that device to a computer or network.

We've seen **botnets**, **keyloggers**, **phishers**, **smishers**, and **vishers**. Now come the **podslurpers**. The last two decades have seen an explosion of terms relating to hi-tech fraud. The new terminology is often as ingenious as the measures produced to counteract them. There are, it seems, marauders waiting at the edge of every network for the one vulnerable machine that will become their key with which to enter and steal valuable data.

A botnet, firstly, is a collection of software 'robots' which run autonomously under a common control infrastructure. It is the weapon of choice for 'cybergangs' who commit fraud. Such criminals propagate viruses or spyware which are downloaded onto unprotected computers. At a designated time, the infected computers bombard a chosen target with junk data until it eventually collapses.

Sniffing, or **keylogging**, is the practice of recording every keystroke a computer user makes by secretly installing a special program. The results are used to gain access to a user's password and other private details in order to commit **cyber-heists**.

Spear phishing, meanwhile, is a highly targeted form of 'phishing', the fraudulent practice of sending emails from an apparently trusted source requesting personal information such as passwords. Unlike standard phishing, in which emails are sent to a general population via widespread spam emails, spear phishers target just one organization.

polyclinics

large medical facilities which bring GPs and consultants together under one roof, together with services traditionally delivered by hospitals.

In early 2008, Lord Darzi of Denham, charged by the government with the task of reviewing Britain's NHS, spoke on BBC One's *Breakfast* programme about a future in which 'we are going to see a critical mass of general practitioners working together, rather than what we used to see in the past which were practices with a single-handed clinician'.

Lord Darzi was speaking about **polyclinics**, new and large 'super-practices' which would house GPs together with other health professionals such as consultants, psychiatrists, and podiatrists. The majority would be formed by dissolving several existing GP surgeries and housing the doctors under one roof, while bringing in other expertise with the aim of offering some social, complementary, and hospital services alongside the traditional ones. The measure would, Lord Darzi believes, deliver better and more coherent healthcare.

The government-backed plans for such centres have come under sustained criticism from medical experts, who claim that they have been found to offer poorer choice and access than surgery-based GPs and that the personal bond that exists between doctor and patient would be eroded. Moreover, they say, GPs are expert generalists: to break medical care down into a spectrum of specialisms would undermine that holistic and generalized service.

If the new London Mayor Boris Johnson also spoke out against it, the polyclinic concept is not without its proponents. While some newspapers decided that a healthcare system that is used in Russia justified shock headlines such as 'GPs' leader hits out at plans for Soviet-style "polyclinics"' (*The Observer*), others defended what David Aaronovitch, writing in *The Times*, called 'an epistemological break', but nonetheless a good one. 'I would like a relationship, but I would much prefer an expert. It is all very well for a newspaper to caption a cosy GP photo with the words "The family doctor: the cornerstone of personal, continuous patient care"; the question is how good this continuous care is.'

It is perhaps worth noting that the term 'polyclinics' is generally used by the government and those who back the measure. Opponents tend to prefer the hyperbole of **superclinics** or **supersurgeries** in their comments. It may not be too long before **überclinics** get a mention.

pond swooping

a form of competitive parachuting in which participants touch down on a surface of water and glide across it until they reach the shore.

Pond swooping is also known as **extreme skydiving**, a term which perhaps more accurately reflects this new sport's challenges. The swoopers must land in the water only partially in order to be able to glide across it: no mean feat when they are hurtling towards the ground at an even higher speed than is involved in regular dives.

If water is unavailable, there is also land swooping, where fields of corn or other crops provide a (relatively) soft area over which the divers can brush their feet as they glide.

The longest swoop on record is held by Canadian Jay Moledzki, who swooped 678.15ft in Colorado.

No wonder it is being billed as the ultimate high (for spectators as well as those who dare to do it).

Poolates™

an exercise programme which combines the principles of
Pilates with an aquatic workout.

Poolates is one of the latest fitness programmes to arrive on our
physical and linguistic doorstep. A blend of 'pool' and 'Pilates',
it claims to offer a high-quality strength-building programme which
enhances posture, flexibility, and muscle strength. The adoption of
the Pilates principles means that it targets the deep postural muscles
and emphasizes natural movements and breathing.

Such is the popularity of Pilates that it has spawned numerous
adaptations aimed at specific audiences. Poolates is just one
of several variations which incorporate the principles of other
exercise programmes. The trend is there on the aquatic side too,
with **aqua-chi** (t'ai chi in the water), **aqua-jogging**, and
aqua-gym (a system, including a sub-aqua rowing machine and
step-climber, that is lowered into the pool and attached via giant
suction pads) all having had a look-in over recent years. But it is
Pilates-based fusion regimes that are making the headlines,
including **Yogilates**, **Cardiolates** (involving trampolining for
improved cardiovascular health), and **Plus-Size Pilates** for
larger-sized people. The exercise versions, you might say, of
musical 'mash-ups'.

The generation of spin-off terms, however short-lived, is one
of the key criteria for a word's survival. Pilates' place in the
dictionary seems for now as ensured as it is in our gyms and
sports centres.

If Poolates may seem a whimsical idea to some and a passing fad to others,
a look back to earlier fashionable kinds of exercise may at least reassure
that fitness crazes are nothing new. They include **eurhythmics**, popular in

the 1920s and especially promoted by the wonderfully-named Women's League of Health and Beauty.

The *Oxford English Dictionary*, which dates 'eurhythmics' from 1912, defines it as 'a system of rhythmical bodily movements, especially dancing exercises, with musical accompaniment, frequently used for educational purposes'. The Dictionary's first quote, from the *Standard* on 27 November 1912, runs: 'Eurythmics [sic] is no longer a mysterious art – it is the new craze. Eurythmics is a word which Professor Jacques-Dalcroze has invented to describe his "rhythmic gymnastics".'

Eurhythmics clearly caught on very quickly: *The Times* of 13 November 1913 describes a demonstration by Jacques-Dalcroze and his gymnasts at King's Hall in Covent Garden. After 'a number of able pupils' had illustrated the exercise, 'huge delight was caused when . . . a self-sacrificing gentleman from the audience was inveigled into performing some of the simpler exercises, to show how difficult they really were.'

However, eurhythmics were not without controversy: eleven years later, a column in the same newspaper was excitingly headlined 'Eurhythmics in Church. U.S. Rector defies Bishop'. The article recounts how the rector of a church in the diocese of New York had persisted in 'including in the services rhythmic dances by bare-footed girls despite his (Bishop Manning's) interdiction'. The Bishop's view was that 'last Sunday Dr Cuthrie definitely challenged the Bishop's authority by these eurhythmics, the repetition of which his superior had forbidden.'

For all its novelty, one can't quite see that happening with Poolates.

popcorn lung

a potentially lethal lung complaint caused, it is believed,
by the inhalation of a flavouring ingredient in popcorn.

In late 2007 news emerged of the first consumer case linked to
popcorn lung. The first-known incidence of the illness
outside popcorn factory employees was reported in a man who ate
over two bags of the food daily but who had to stop because of the
damage it was causing to his health.

Popcorn lung is believed to be caused by the flavouring diacetyl,
which gives popcorn its buttery taste. As a result of prolonged
exposure to it, the small airways known as the bronchials become
scarred and inflamed. The disease has been known among factory
workers, some of whom have needed lung transplants, while others
have died.

Even before news of the first popcorn-eater falling victim to
the disease became public, popcorn manufacturers had begun
to take action, including an outright ban on the use of diacetyl.
Meanwhile, lawyers specializing in popcorn lung litigation were
already advertising their services on the Web, in between headlines
such as 'You butter believe it'. For those afflicted by the life-
threatening disease, however, and for the champions of slow food
rather than microwave convenience, it is a deadly serious affair.

potwalloping

the practice by local people in Northam, Devon, of holding back coastal erosion by gathering twice a year to replace by hand the stones of a unique pebble ridge which have been washed away.

Potwalloping is a wonderful example of an ancient term which is brought back into currency thanks to one newspaper's report and the subsequent discussions of it across chat forums and news sites.

A 'potwalloper' or 'potwaller' was at one time a householder with his own separate fireplace on which a pot could be boiled. As a result of this he was granted the vote in some parliamentary constituencies, before the Reform Act of 1832 was passed. In later years, potwalloping denoted a Devonian custom whereby householders of the borough of Northam – the 'potwallopers' – would throw onto a ridge pebbles that had been washed down, in order to protect their grazing rights. The result became a pebble ridge that is a unique geological structure.

Potwalloping ceased when members of England's oldest golf club in Northam Burrows were banned by a government agency from the annual practice of rebuilding the offshore ridge, which Natural England perceives as an interference with nature on a Site of Special Interest. Yet potwalloping is considered by locals as an essential measure to limit erosion of the dunes. As a result of a ban, they believe, the Northam Burrows golf course will disappear into the sea.

Undeterred by the ban, the nearby village of Westward Ho! held its annual Potwalloping Festival, traditionally the time when
112 locals repaired the ridge after the winter storms but now a lively celebration of the start of summer.

purrcast

a downloadable broadcast of a cat purring (blend of
'purr' + 'podcast').

Purrcasts (and **purrblogs**) are the latest in a long and
varied line of idiosyncratic 'podcasts' (see below), **designed
to be downloaded onto a computer or an MP3 player for others to
hear. The cat community regularly share information about their
pets' personalities and habits, and have the audio and video to
prove it. Many an online testimony praises the soothing quality of
an extended purr.**

Other sonorous and non-human broadcasts include
whalecasts, **horsecasts**, and, of course, **dogcasts**.

One of the great winners of the last decade, both linguistically and
technologically, is **podcasting**. Defined as the broadcasting or
downloading of audio broadcasts onto an MP3 player, it is a portmanteau
word, a blend of 'iPod' and 'broadcasting'.

Like another hugely successful blend, 'blog', 'podcast' quickly generated
a subset of associated words, thereby proving its staying power as a
neologism. **Mommycasting** denotes programmes made by and aimed at
mothers; **couplecasting** is a programme presented by a couple and which
often discusses relationship issues; while **Godcasting** is the broadcasting
or downloading of religious content. **Vodcasting** and **blogcasting**
are video and blog broadcasts made available for downloading.
Slivercasting, meanwhile, is online broadcasting which is able to target
a small audience (a 'sliver' of the overall viewing base) – as opposed to
silvercasting, which is programming for the increasingly time-rich retired.

Rickrolling

an Internet 'meme' whereby a web user is unexpectedly taken to a video of the 1980s pop song 'Never Gonna Give You Up' by Rick Astley.

Rickrolling has become a global phenomenon. An Internet meme refers to something that spreads very quickly across the Internet, and this one certainly did that. If you are **Rickrolled**, you are the 'victim' of a highly infectious (in web terms) prank known as a **bait and switch**, whereby a web link which looks entirely in keeping with the content being viewed is actually a façade for a link to Rick Astley's number one hit.

A poll carried out in the US estimated that over 18 million Americans had been Rickrolled. Many of them fell into the April Fool's trap set up by the video-sharing site *YouTube*, which made every single video link on its home page a Rickroll. It is unsurprising, then, that the song is about to be re-released for official listening. 'Never Gonna Give You Up' proved a highly accurate description of what it felt like to be Rickrolled over and over.

Rickrolling is a descendant of an older Internet joke, known as **duckrolling**, in which unsuspecting viewers would be offered one link and sent instead to a picture of a duck on wheels (hence the 'roll').

In a wonderful collision of two recent cultural phenomena, there are also Rickroll **flashmobs** – gatherings organized by real or virtual word of mouth in which groups collect in a public place and perform something unusual for a brief time before briefly dispersing. Cities across Britain and the US have been Rickrolled: people have gathered to lip-synch the hit at London train stations and New York basketball games. The participants stick faithfully to the style of the video, in which the baby-faced Astley, dressed in high-waisted 80s jeans and a denim shirt, sways from side to side.

If, in the words of one organizer, your grandmother hasn't been Rickrolled, 'she will soon. And be singing along'.

run-off

a second ballot, following a previously indecisive election.

The *Oxford English Dictionary*'s first citation for a **run-off** in this context is from 1873, and is defined as 'a final deciding race held after a dead heat'. From the early 20th century, however, the meaning shifted somewhat, and is defined as 'an election held to decide the issue between the two candidates who gained the largest number of votes in a previous indecisive election'. While most of the evidence from the next few decades relates to US politics, *The New York Times* of 7 December 1965 ran the headline: 'De Gaulle silent on whether he will enter run-off'.

In 2008, the term became almost synonymous with events in Zimbabwe, where the results of the presidential election were delayed for weeks in spite of clear indications that the opposition Movement for Democratic Change, led by Morgan Tsvangirai, had defeated the incumbent Robert Mugabe by some margin. When the official count was declared, amid international protests over its reliability, the count was declared too close for call, necessitating a run-off between the two candidates in late June. That run-off never happened.

Like the term 'first-past-the-post', a run-off originated in the world of sport. The electoral cleansing of Zimbabwe was a very long way from being a fair game.

Electoral cleansing takes as its model the **ethnic cleansing** of Yugoslavia's civil war. Meaning the use of force and intimidation to remove or prevent people who are likely to vote against a regime, it has been used since the mid 1990s but came back into daily currency with the stifling in Zimbabwe of anti-government and anti-Mugabe activity.

schwag

1. a type of low-grade marijuana.
2. a company giveaway.

According to a post in the online slang lexicon of the *Urban Dictionary*, **schwag** is 'cannabis of very, very low potency and quality, usually harvested too early or too late in the growing cycle'. Often associated with marijuana that has been smuggled across the Mexican border, it is cheaper than higher-grade and higher-potency forms of the drug.

The *Urban Dictionary* also tells us that some varieties of 'schwag' are known as **dirt**, given their resemblance to dry and crumbly compost.

'**S**chwag' also has an extended use, as a figurative expression for company giveaways (and as an alternative – some say Yiddish-accented – version of 'swag'). **Schwag bags** are apparently all the commercial rage: according to the technology magazine *Wired*, 'A monkey screen-wipe! A crumb-sweeper car! A foam cell phone-chair! Today's schwag industry, 450,000 products strong, may soon double in size.'

A study by one of today's leading chroniclers of slang, Jonathon Green, of half a millennium's worth of collected material – amounting to almost 100,000 words and phrases – shows the extent to which the same themes recur. Looking at the current slang lexicon, and besides sex, music, and money, it is drugs and drug-taking that are the most productive generators of what has been called 'language with its sleeves rolled up'.

Many of these terms are euphemistic. The subjects which invite euphemism vary according to our times and preoccupations – and, of course, according to the prevailing requirements of political correctness. If the 18th century saw a strong need to tiptoe around gin, creating a wonderful cocktail of terms in the process (including 'strip-me-naked', 'tiger's milk', and 'royal bob'), today it is the drug lexicon that needs similar camouflage. Cannabis alone can be **blonde**, **cheeba**, **bullyon**, **jolly green**, **bazooka**, **chronic**, **dank**, **mota**, **ganga**, and **Buddha**.

scuppie

an acronym for a 'socially conscious upwardly-mobile person/urban professional'.

The **scuppie** is the latest in the lexicon of demographic groups, coined to describe an urban professional who is socially conscious. As far back as 1988, *The Sydney Morning Herald* placed the scuppie alongside the **bobo** ('burnt-out but opulent'), but the term has since come back into currency thanks to the ascendancy of our worries about our environmental footprint. So, for example, today's scuppie might be interested in the 'Bamboo' phone, powered by a wind-up mechanism.

Interestingly, the scuppie of yesterday could also be a 'senior citizen yuppie'. It is a perfect example of how words change to fit our new requirements. Today's version, however, is entirely green:

'I'm not a true scuppie – a Socially Conscious Upwardly Mobile Person – because newspaper people are not so much upwardly mobile as backwardly noble. I can't afford to blow the rent money at Whole Foods on organic cruelty-free hand-churned onion dip or imported free-trade hemp dental floss.'
(Samantha Bennett, 'How green is my footprint?', *Pittsburgh Post-Gazette*, 24 April 2008.)

shoefiti

the hanging of shoes, especially trainers, over telephone
wires.

For most Britons the sight of a pair of trainers hanging over a
telephone wire might raise an eyebrow or two, or be dismissed
as a harmless teenage prank. According to the *Mail on Sunday*, in
an article in April 2007, the manifestation should be taken as a
sign of something far more sinister. For affluent residents of a
certain London suburb, one of the first British spots to witness
the established US phenomenon of **shoefiti**, it was 'a sign of
something far more sinister. It tells them violent gangs are
operating in their midst'.

For the *Mail*, shoefiti is a part of gang culture and a symbol from
one clan to another to keep off their patch. Ask an American,
however, and they will dismiss this as an urban myth. For the real
origins of the shoefiti idea remain a mystery, much as the
'installation' itself – the flinging of the shoes over the wire – is done
in secret, often in the dead of night.

Many theories have, of course, been offered as to shoefiti's
origins. Some suggest a military basis, when combat boots
were thrown over a power line to mark the end of active duty. Others
believe it marks other rites of passage, from romantic conquests to
university graduation. The term itself is said to have been coined
by Ed Kohler, a Minneapolis resident who began to notice shoes
hanging from power lines near his home. He set up *Shoefiti.com*
in 2005.

Wherever it came from, the phenomenon of shoefiti may have
firmly crossed the Atlantic. If the sight of a pair of trainers in

The Simpsons Movie is anything to go by, this new kind of environmental graffiti is also very much a part of popular culture.

How do new words come about? While most of us like to think of mint-new coinages as the inspiration of a moment, in fact only about 1% of them are entirely new, and of those an even smaller percentage are conjured up out of thin air. The vast majority are born of processes which build on existing words in some way. Of these, 'blending' is one of the most productive – and entertaining.

Blending is the combination of existing words, or parts of words. Among the colourful results from recent years are **frienemy** (a fair-weather friend), **ladults** (a man laddish in behaviour but able to show maturity when required), **Wiimote** (a motion-sensitive remote control used with the cult Nintendo Wii video game), and **peerents** (parents who try to be their children's friends). **Shoefiti**, a blend of 'shoe' and 'graffiti', now joins the club.

'Shoefiti' is unusual in that, although the result of blending, it looks to be the creation of one person and can be traced back to a particular moment in time. Such certainty is rare for any lexicographer, who can usually pinpoint the rough period in which a word emerged but for whom its exact time and place of birth is most often elusive.

In shoefiti's case it is also clear *why* the neologism was born: precisely because it was needed. It is an excellent example of a word needing to be found in order to describe an existing phenomenon. That shoefiti was around before its naming is clear. Take the following account, from *The Intelligencer* (Doylestown, Pennsylvania) in 1996:

'As I sat outside, two guys were playing a rugged game of playground basketball. Overhead, pairs of old basketball shoes dangled from telephone lines. In this neighborhood, when a basketball player's favorite pair of shoes wears out, he tosses them on the telephone line. This, I was told, is the player's way of saluting a good pair of shoes. It is also a way of marking turf. Sitting outside Pat's with the sneakers dangling above me and a cheese steak in front of me, I felt like I was experiencing the real Philadelphia.'

A linguistic gap, indeed. 'Shoefiti' may well beat the odds facing every new word and stick around. Certainly as long as shoes find their way onto telephone wires, it will need to.

shopdropping

a reverse form of shoplifting in which products are left in stores rather than taken out, as a form of social/political protest.

To **shopdrop** is to make a statement about commercialism, and to try to subvert it: in other words, it is a form of what has become known as **cultural jamming**. In most cases, the 'artist' replaces a product on a shop shelf with one of their own that features a political or social message. Recently, however, in a kind of double subversion, the concept has itself become a commercial one: local bands and artists are leaving behind copies of their albums as a means of promoting them. This is **shopdropping** at its most literal. The following two quotes give some idea of the two extremes:

'Similar to the way street art stakes a claim to public space for self expression, my shopdropping project subverts commercial space for artistic use in an attempt to disrupt the mundane commercial process with a purely artistic moment.'
(Ryan Watkins-Hughes, on *shopdropping.net*, 26 December 2007.)

'At Mac's Backs Paperbacks, a used bookstore in Cleveland Heights, Ohio, employees are dealing with the influx of shopdropped works by local poets and playwrights by putting a price tag on them and leaving them on the shelves.'
(*The New York Times*, 24 December 2007.)

showa

a slang term for 'good', particularly in Liverpool.

For some Liverpudlians, their home town is **Showapool**. To be **showa** is to be like the new version of 'sick' (surfer slang that has gone mainstream and, like so much of slang in its good/bad inversion, means 'great'): in other words it is all good.

sleevefacing

the posting of a personal photo on the *Facebook* website with one's face obscured by an album cover, arranged to create a visual illusion.

Sleevefacing is the latest in the lexicon that is being generated by social networking sites at rapid speed (see the verb **facebook**). The vast membership size of sites such as *Facebook* means that users strive for individuality in their own personal space in order to stand out from the crowd. In this case, the capturing of personal images behind a favourite album cover artwork has produced some wonderful (and some curious) results.

The idea is said to have been created by DJs who consider vinyl records to be far cooler than CDs and who started a craze of spinning turntables while holding an album cover in front of them. A piece in *The Observer* in February 2008 gives an idea of the possibilities:

'Some snap sophisticated group portraits or domestic tableaus in which ever greater numbers of sleeves are cleverly incorporated. Others attempt to use two gatefold sleeves, or tricky little seven-inch single or CD covers, or just turn to Bookfacing, which makes them look more intellectual, literally. But some drink one too many Stellas and find themselves producing 'sleeverotica'. Musical artistes who've ever displayed their bottoms or open mouths on album sleeves will likely find themselves shuddering this year.'

slow medicine

medical care which focuses on patient comfort rather than aggressive treatments.

Based on research undertaken by the Dartmouth Medical School in the US, **slow medicine** takes the premise that attempts to tackle conditions aggressively may not be a patient's best option, particularly when they may not be treatable and are the result of old age. As an article in *The New York Times* put it, 'slow medicine encourages physicians to put on the brakes when considering care that may have high risks and limited rewards . . . and it educates patients and families how to push back against emergency room trips and hospitalizations'.

If the fast medicine alternative is all about cure and dramatic intervention, the slow kind is all about comfort.

The benefits of taking things slowly are behind the ethos of other recently-proposed lifestyle movements, including **slow food**, which emphasizes traditional methods of food production and preparation and the appreciation of fine cuisine. **Slow travel**, meanwhile, is a way of seeing the world without rushing from one destination to another by as fast a means as possible. **Slow shopping** and **slow design** have recently joined the list. They speak for themselves.

The cult of speed that the last few decades have been building up to may yet be tempered by the praise of the slow.

speed mentoring

a style of career- or life-coaching modelled on speed dating, in which each participant has a few minutes to seek advice on career-related questions.

'**S**peed dating? That's so 2003.' Thus declared the 31 March 2008 edition of the Canadian paper *The Globe and Mail*, over a report of a new way of 'jump-starting your destiny'. Not speed dating, then, but its latest spin-off, **speed mentoring**.

Speed-mentoring fairs are thriving across the US and are fast becoming the must-attend events for those aspiring to improve their prospects.

The *Globe and Mail* journalist Rebecca Dube described the process thus: 'When the bell rings, dozens of strangers pair off and size each other up. They shake hands and start talking about life goals, past experiences and future dreams. Some feel a spark, while others suffer through awkward silences. A few minutes later, the bell clangs again and they move on to the next potentially life-changing stranger.'

Although the goals are very different – a new career, not a new romance – the underlying ethos and practicalities behind speed mentoring are very much the same as its dating sibling. Advice today is available everywhere – be it from life coaches, in-company mentor schemes, or online consultancies. Why waste time and money, the argument goes, exploring each avenue when speed mentoring can give you vastly higher odds of finding the right person in one hit?

At a time when the business community regularly gets a bad press for its reliance on jargon, 'speed mentoring' may have the

127

right linguistic verve to win over the cynics. It surely sounds a lot more exciting than the other name it goes under: 'facilitated networking'.

The first **speed-dating** events took place in the late 1990s: those in Pete's Café in Beverly Hills are said to have set the precedent that was then followed across the US. Its portrayal in such programmes as *Sex and the City* no doubt gave an extra boost to something that had already captured the singleton's zeitgeist.

Spin-offs were inevitable. In 2007 **read-dating** parties gave soulmate-searchers a new opportunity. Here, instead of personal details, it is books that the attendees discuss. The principle is the same: literary choices are exchanged with a prospective date for three minutes before the bell rings and seats are swapped for the next conversation.

Rumour has it that **feed dating** may be the next thing to arrive. A bit of linguistic fun maybe, but no one can argue with the success of the format.

speedriding

a new sport which combines skiing, hang-gliding, and sky-diving.

Speedriding has been taking the Alps by storm in recent months. Developed over the last few years in an effort to up the ante in extreme sports still further, it involves skiing with small parachute 'wings' which enable participants to jump or fly over impassable slopes or crevasses at high speed.

It was the film *Playground*, an action skiing and snowboard film, which brought speedriding to wider attention. When footage of two Swiss athletes pushing off the summit of the Eiger was broadcast on *YouTube* and other online video sites, it was put firmly on the mainstream map of extreme sport.

'The two men push off . . . , ski up to the cliff edge, and jump into thin air. In Leicester Square, the audience watching the footage on a huge cinema screen emit a collective gasp. For while film of skiers doing daring jumps has become so commonplace as to lose much of its impact, this is something totally new'.
(Isobel Rostron in *The Observer*, February 2008.)

T5

the abbreviation given to Heathrow's new Terminal 5.

If 'A1' is the signifier of excellence, then **T5**, in 2008, became the mark of anything but. On the day that Heathrow's new £4.3 billion terminal opened, cancelled flights and a meltdown of the baggage system caused a national uproar.

British Airways, which has sole use of the terminal, and BAA, the airport's operator, put the chaos of the baggage system down to 'teething problems'. By the end of the first week, as flights were still being cancelled and bags sent out to Milan for sorting, the conclusion of passengers and the press was more that it was one of the worst PR blunders in modern history.

The *Mirror* accompanied its daily accounts of the continuing chaos with the epithet 'Terminal of Turmoil', while BA's arch-rivals Virgin Atlantic stuck the boot in by saying that BA had been given a wonderful gift in T5, 'but they couldn't unwrap it properly'.

Whether T5 can shed its associations and return to being a neutral brand remains to be seen. For a few critics it seems likely that it may follow in the path of an earlier formula, also intended to denote excellence: namely Clive Sinclair's C5 car, which never quite recovered from the media's criticism of it from day one.

toff

(usually derogatory) a person from the upper classes.

'**D**oes targeting Tory **toffs** still have traction in British politics?' Thus BBC Radio 4's *Today* programme on 20 May 2008, after the spectacular crash of the Labour Party in the Crewe and Nantwich by-election. The party had waged what many believed tantamount to a class war, by calling the Conservative candidate Edward Timpson and his party leader David Cameron a couple of 'Tory toffs'. If intended to alienate the constituency's electorate by invoking a 150-year-old (and loaded) term, the move had clearly – and dramatically – backfired.

Labour's campaign included the shadowing of Mr Timpson by activists dressed in tailcoats and top hats. Unfortunately for them, it emerged in the course of the campaign that Tamsin Dunwoody, the Labour candidate and daughter of Gwyneth Dunwoody, whose untimely death had triggered the by-election, lived in a house larger than her Tory rival.

'**T**off' was originally a term, given by the lower classes, to a person who was stylishly dressed or who had a smart appearance. Henry Mayhew, in his *London Labour and the London Poor*, quotes one street observer from 1851: 'If it's a lady and a gentleman, then we cries, "A toff and a doll!" ' It was in later years that the term took on its fully disparaging tone. Its origins are in the 'tuft' that adorned the mortar boards of Oxford and Cambridge scholars, who were usually noblemen or 'gentlemen commoners'.

English is full of the resonances of class. Some of the most successful terms are born in humour, as in **nice-but-dim**, a designator of someone who is incompetent if utterly good-natured, and popularized by Tim Nice-But-Dim, the good-natured, upper-class simpleton in the BBC series *Harry Enfield's Television Programme*.

The rebel Conservative MP Julian Critchley used to write somewhat satirically about traditional landed fellow Tories as 'Knights of the Shires'. The wonderfully-named Sir Tufton Beamish was the probable model of *Private Eye*'s 'Sir Bufton Tufton', regularly lampooned as a stereotype of the great British political toff.

Lord Snooty is one of the most memorable fictional toffs, who appeared with his Pals in the UK comic *The Beano* for over 50 years. In May 2008 Toby Young wrote in *The Guardian* of the likely repercussions for him of Boris Johnson's accession to the London mayorship:

'This has led me to reconsider my position on the "Hon" question. I haven't used my title since the late 1980s, reasoning that it would harm my career as a journalist, but if Cameron wins the next general election, it may be time to dust it off and start displaying it again. Instead of dismissing me as a member of the lucky sperm club, my superiors would treat me with new-found respect, assuming I had a direct line to Lord Snooty and his pals in Downing Street.'

treggings

trousers that fit very tightly, in the style of leggings (blend of 'trousers' + 'leggings').

Treggings were heralded as one of the latest catwalk trends in the 2007–8 fashion season. Essentially trousers which are so tight they look just like leggings, they left fashion commentators asking just how wearable they could be by the average Briton.

*T*he Sun offered wannabe tregging-buyers some style tips, including the avoidance of block colours or vertical lines 'unless your legs are VERY good', and 'if you're curvy wear with long tops to hide a muffin top and keep the look long and lean'. That way, the paper's young fashion panel concluded, we could avoid looking like the 'pram-pushing Vicky Pollards of this world'.

In fact, while most trendsetting fashionistas judged 'treggings' to be a ridiculous word, the trouser-legging hybrid found its way into the wardrobes of many a chic celebrity. Kate Moss was seen to sport a PVC pair, which was more or less enough in itself to guarantee demand.

Made of a more robust fabric than the original leggings – anything from denim to lurex – treggings may be the latest incarnation of the ever-popular skinny jeans. Moreover, the spray-on trousers of the punk era may be getting a second run for their money, even if those now sporting treggings would positively shudder at the thought.

The vocabulary of fashion necessarily moves fast. It doesn't, however, always move in a straight line: just as trends come and go and then come back again, so do the fashion terms that describe them. **Capri pants**, **clamdiggers** (both calf-length trousers for women), **kitten heels**, and

basques, **baguettes**, **bandeaus**, and **boob tubes** (loaf-shaped handbags and strapless tops) have all re-entered our vocabulary in recent years as their look has returned to hipness.

Not all fashion-speak, then, is new. Treggings, however, are. A 'portmanteau' word that combines 'trousers' and 'leggings', it sits alongside (linguistically at least) such recent creations as **tankinis** (also known as **kamikinis**: swimming costumes which combine a camisole top with a bikini bottom), **binikis** (a support device for the buttocks that gives them a firm shape), and **tuxedas** (tuxedos for women).

Mixing and matching is clearly as cool linguistically as it is sartorially.

umbilicoplasty

a surgical procedure which transforms a belly button.

In recent months plastic surgeons have been reporting a spike in the graph of a hitherto relatively rare procedure: navel reconstruction, which may for example turn an **innie** to an **outie**, is what *The New York Times* described as 'final proof of the midriff's total cultural triumph'.

Having been hidden away for years, the navel is now an essential part of fashion. Stomach-baring tops and bottom-hugging trousers are designed to give it maximum exposure, enhanced with the very latest in 'belly rings'. According to a study included in the *New York Times* report, about a third of American students now have navel piercings. The search for the 'Ideal Female Umbilicus' (the title of a lecture at the University of Missouri) is apparently now on.

The navel aesthetic is not of course new. It is classically associated with exoticism and the mystical aspects of birth and life. In Indian culture, a dimpled navel is considered a special asset of any prospective bride. For many, however, surgery which is determined by a fashion choice is taking things too far. The body plastic, it seems, now reigns supreme.

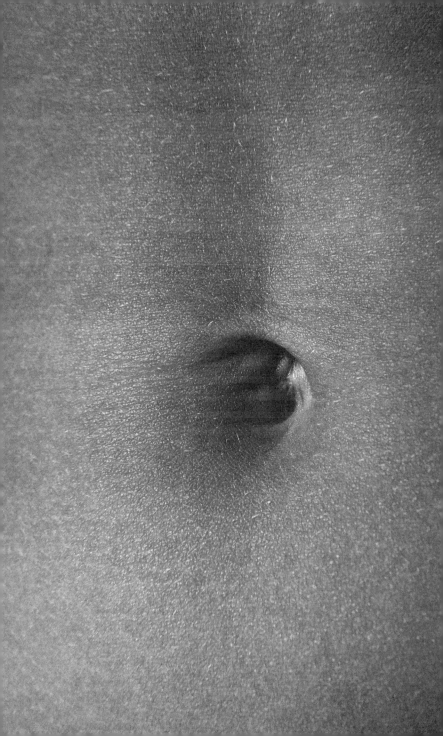

undo-plasty

surgery to rectify bad plastic surgery.

The need for reversing cosmetic surgery which has gone very wrong is apparently gathering momentum. According to a survey by the British Association of Aesthetic Plastic Surgeons, over 33% of surgeons have carried out an unprecedented number of corrective operations in the last five years. This **undo-plasty** is the result, the Association surmises, of 'cheap cosmetic surgery holidays'.

The Guardian cites as an example 'Katie Price, who has been steadily dismantling her alter ego, Jordan. Just before Christmas, the glamour model had her breasts reduced from her previously well-known 32FFs, and her lips also looked somewhat deflated.' Courtney Love is said to want to go back to 'the mouth God gave me'. Women are apparently opting for the removal of breast implants, and the reversal of rhinoplasty (nose jobs). Men too are opting for the 'back to nature' look, and having hair plugs removed.

Ironically, what all this doesn't mean is a backlash against surgery itself. All the statistics suggest that this is still on the rise, and that the corrective operations simply add one more procedure to a lifetime's rapidly extending list.

vuvuzela

an air-horn or trumpet sounded by South African football fans.

According to most who describe it, the sound of **vuvuzelas** en masse is exactly like an elephant. The instrument has come to symbolize football in South Africa and was the focus of much attention during the 2008 African Cup of Nations.

The vuvuzela is already a sporting icon in its home nation. When FIFA announced in 2004 that South Africa is to host the 2010 World Cup, sales shot up, with reportedly 20,000 sold on the day.

It is said that the first vuvuzela was the 'kudu' horn, made from the African antelope and used to summon villagers to a meeting. As to its linguistic origin, there are numerous theories. Some say it comes from the Zulu for 'making noise'. Others suggest it comes from the slang of the townships and is related to the word 'shower', perhaps because it showers its listeners with music or, more cynically, looks a little like a shower head.

Today's vuvuzelas are made in plastic and coloured according to team strips. They each carry a warning about blowing in a neighbouring fan's ear. This capacity for deafening noise has made a few enemies: a *News24* journalist described it as 'an instrument of hell', while the South African Football Association has asked for manufacturers to make modifications to the vuvuzela's weight for fear that it may be used as an offensive weapon.

Football's beautiful noise it may not be, but together with the **makarapa**, a decorated form of miner's helmet which sports a team's logo and colour, the vuvuzela is now part of any self-respecting South African supporter's arsenal.

wavefarm

a machine for producing energy from the waves of the sea.

In early October 2007, *The Guardian* reported on two very different kind of weather-watchers, gathered off the coast of northern Portugal. While the surfers hoped for high waves and choppy seas, a group of engineers and businessmen were hoping for the very opposite: smooth calm seas on which to launch the latest venture in renewable energy, the world's first **wavefarm**.

The machines in question are known as 'Pelamis', Latin for 'sea snake'. They have been developed by a Scottish company and have the appearance of a series of snake-like red tubes, linked together and pointing in the same direction as the sea's waves. As the waves travel through the tubes, the momentum of the water causes them to move up and down, generating in doing so an energy which can then be harnessed by means of a hydraulic system. The energy produced – in the form of electricity – is then pumped into the national grid.

The wavefarm is a financial risk: its first years will be far from profitable, and the investment is necessarily long-term. It was the Portuguese government that recognized the potential and which gave one of the newest renewable energy fields its first opportunity.

The wavefarm has not been without setbacks, both technological and meteorological. The ambition of Enersis, the company behind it, is nonetheless to have several hundred machines floating off the same coastline, enough eventually to light up 350,000 homes.

webcom

a daily online interactive sitcom with content scripted by viewers.

First there was the sitcom, then the romcom and the zomromcom*. Now there is the **webcom**, a new genre of sitcom in which viewers can interact from their computers, and even direct the script.

In the summer of 2007, a media company co-founded by Steve Coogan, the comic writer and comedian behind such successes as *Knowing Me, Knowing You . . . with Alan Partridge* and *The Mighty Boosh*, announced *Where are the Joneses?*, a sitcom to be broadcast in two five-minute episodes each day to which viewers could contribute via so-called Wikidot technology: a multi-user web environment based on 'wiki' technology (see below). They were also able to share comments and catch up on storylines via social networking sites such as *Facebook*, *Twitter* feeds on their mobile phone (a free service allowing short text-based posts called 'tweets' via instant messaging), and video-sharing links on *YouTube*. In short, this would be a sitcom on an unprecedentedly democratic and collaborative scale.

Where are the Joneses? had mixed reviews. In practice, the interactivity proved difficult to manage, and ideas submitted by viewers were only seldom taken up. Nevertheless, the webcom concept attracted hundreds of blog comments and reviews. The idea of a TV programme that can be freely re-edited was one that clearly appealed, and that is likely to be taken up again before too long.

* a romantic comedy featuring zombies.

In April 2004, *The Guardian* carried an interview with Ward Cunningham, an American computer programmer who was the developer of the first **wiki**. Taking its name from the phrase 'wiki wiki' in Hawaiian, meaning 'very quick', a wiki is a website that can be edited by anyone, and on which the processes of editing and reading are linked, thus avoiding the need for continuous uploading. The best known is *Wikipedia*, a comprehensive online encyclopedia which is written collaboratively by volunteers from across the globe: any visitor can contribute their own definition.

Ward Cunningham described a wiki as 'a process for organizing and explaining experience. Wiki provides the machinery for weaving together those stories. It's a natural, social thing.' Thanks to the success of sites such as *Wikipedia* and *Wiktionary*, the term 'wiki' has cemented itself not just in English – it is now included in dictionaries of current English – but in many other languages too. When *Where are the Joneses?* was announced, press articles featured the term without explanation, in confident recognition of its currency.

Alongside 'wiki', 'web-' has been a rather more predictably popular prefix in the 2000s. **Webumentaries**, online documentaries, **webisodes**, episodes of TV shows that are available as Internet downloads, and **webcasts**, media files distributed over the Internet (essentially, Internet broadcasts), have all made an appearance in the last decade. And, of course, the **webcam** (on which the 'webcom' plays) is the parent of hundreds of 'cam' spin-offs: including the more unusual **cowcams** (on *MooTube*), **hencams** (with which egg buyers can reassure themselves of the producing hen's welfare), **shark-** and **jelly cams**, and a **paint cam** (where you can quite literally watch paint dry). And, on *Countdown*, there is of course the **pencam**.

WiMax

a digital communications system that provides wireless Internet access over long distances. An acronym for Worldwide Interoperability for Microwave Access.

WiMax is a supersized Wi-Fi, the most popular wireless technology. Its technology has the power to give whole cities Internet coverage: and Milton Keynes already has it.

Unlike Wi-Fi technology, WiMax can offer high-speed Internet access over very long distances instead of just a few metres. It also has the potential to usher in a new age of full Internet connectivity on mobile phones.

In spite of its capabilities, however, WiMax is not widely used. Users need expensive hardware, whilst Wi-Fi is built into increasing numbers of desktop computers, laptops, and mobile phones. Thanks to a new technology called **HSDPA** (High Speed Downlink Packet Access), which only requires a software upgrade to get it working, mobile third-generation phone companies are also able to offer high-speed web access.

Nonetheless, experts believe we are going to be hearing a lot more about WiMax in the near future. Milton Keynes may seem an unlikely global hot spot for groundbreaking technology, but it may yet revolutionize city life. That said, Britain has some way to go before rivalling Pakistan, which has the largest fully-functioning WiMax network in the world.

YAOI

a type of manga (comic), originally Japanese, that focuses on male-to-male sexual relationships.

The genre of **YAOI** comics, like the manga itself, originated in Japan in the late 1970s. It began primarily to parody existing publications, but it has since developed its own style and its own following outside Japan and particularly in the US. In fact, the preferred term for the genre in Japan itself is now **BL**, an abbreviation of 'boy love'.

If they are growing in popularity, YAOIs, unlike mangas in general which have a huge following outside Japan as well as within it, are still on the fringes of the comic industry. They are, however, getting noticed. A recent *Washington Post* article concluded that 'If Jack London and A.N. Roquelaure (Anne Rice's erotic avatar) had been commissioned to write a novel that would appeal simultaneously to lovers of yaoi (X-rated manga featuring gay men and favored by female readers) and to furries (fans in fur suits who enjoy pretending to be anthropomorphic animals), the result might very well have resembled *A Companion to Wolves*.'

The term is said to be a Japanese acronym formed from the phrase 'yama nashi, ochi nashi, imi nashi', which can be translated into English as 'no peak, no point, no problem'. Some suggest it actually means 'no story, just the good bits' – that is, mostly sex with very little plot.

And Finally . . .

funt

A person whose credit history is so poor that they are unable to get credit.

Funt is probably designed to look and sound like a swear word. It certainly defines something undesirable, for a 'funt' is contraction of 'Financially UNTouchable', and is the latest label for someone in the predicament of being unable to obtain any credit thanks to a very poor credit rating.

In June 2008 the word was given a parliamentary airing, when the British MP Stephen Ladyman brought the plight of funts to the attention of the House. Mr Ladyman believes that everyone should have access to credit, regardless of past financial mistakes. 'Funts should be not ostracised, but helped'.

The word is the coinage of Richard Rubin, who has created a Web site for funts which aims to give advice to those in debt and unable to get help.

As the *Sun* declared, 'it's no fun being a funt'. Given the black clouds gathering over the British economy, many more people may be discovering just that.

John Lewis list

a list itemizing expense allowances for MPs' second homes.

Increased scrutiny of parliamentary allowances from opposition parties and from the public brought in the early summer of 2008 a little-known term into the spotlight. The **John Lewis list**, released into the public domain under the Freedom of Information Act, is the nickname for the collection of household goods that could until recently be claimed by MPs at public expense. The cost allowed for each item was based on prices at the John Lewis department store.

Gordon Brown's plans to abandon the allowances and reform its controversial rules angered many MPs, including 34 government ministers, who voted to reject independent audits of their expense claims and to keep the John Lewis list. New plans drawn up in the wake of the vote ensured both greater scrutiny but also continued allowances on many household goods.

The *Guardian* listed some examples. MPs are allowed to claim up to £10,000 for a new kitchen, more than £6,000 for a bathroom and £750 for a television. They can also claim reimbursement from the taxpayer for stereos worth up to £750, £300 towards air-conditioning units, and £2,000 for a furniture suite for their second homes.

The result, in the view of the Shadow Leader of the House of Commons Theresa May, was a botched job: 'The Government is treating people like fools; they are just replacing the John Lewis list with the Ikea list.'

Brandjacking

The fraudulent use of an Internet domain name that closely resembles that of a well-established brand (blend of brand + hijacking).

The act of **brandjacking** is by now familiar to most Web users. The technique of creating a domain name that uses an existing trademark in order to deceive potential customers is far from new. The exploitation of well-known brands is increasing exponentially, and combatting the problem is proving an enormous challenge.

If the phenomenon is far from new, however, this latest term coined to describe it is. It appeared in June 2008 in a report published by the market analysis firm MarkMonitor, which studied brandjacking incidents affecting 25 top companies, and which concluded that brand abuse on the Web is greater than previously thought.

Brandjacking can encompass a number of online threats, the biggest of which is **cybersquatting**, the unauthorized use of a trademarked name in a Web domain that points visitors to a website that is not owned by the trademark holder. Microsoft, one of the companies studied by MarkMonitor, was found to have reclaimed over 1,000 domain names (such as 1microsoft.67 or freehotmail.net) in the space of only a few months.

The means by which brandjackers avoid prosecution from registered brand owners also has a name: **kiting**, whereby a company registers and uses a domain name for the allowed grace period of five days or less without actually purchasing it. In researching the domain name histories of several firms, MarkMonitor discovered that a few of them are sharing and kiting the same domain names over and over: in other words cybersquatting for free.

146　　See also PODSLURPING.

green jumbo

a non-existent aeroplane invented for the purposes of the government consultation over a third runway at Heathrow.

If BAA, Heathrow airport's operator, didn't have enough headaches after the opening week of T5, in July 2008 it faced more criticism over the **green jumbo** affair. It emerged that the authority created a twin-engine 450 seat 'virtual jet' in order to avoid exceeding the limit set for Heathrow for noise and pollution.

On paper the aeroplane promised to be an environmental saviour. As *The Times* reported: "According to BAA submissions, the green jumbo will account for more flights out of Heathrow by 2030 than four-engined giants such as the double-decker A380, or the new generation of Boeing 747s. It promises to be the world's quietest and cleanest jumbo."

BAA's research was used by the government's transport secretary Ruth Kelly to demonstrate how Heathrow could be expanded without creating more noise or pollution.

There was however, it emerged, one small disadvantage: namely that Airbus and Boeing, the two leading aircraft manufacturers, have no intention of making it. Indeed their experts went so far as to say that such an aircraft was not technically feasible.

The news only increased the criticism of the government for acting as a 'subsidiary of Heathrow'.

The green jumbo may yet become a very large white elephant.

YouTube divorce

the revelation on YouTube of private marital matters during a divorce proceedings in order to humiliate the other party.

'We're the YouTube generation', announced CBS News, 'living in the YouTube Era, in a YouTube World. And now we apparently have a **YouTube Divorce**.' This latter term was propelled into currency thanks to the efforts of the former actress and playwright Tricia Walsh-Smith, who publicly lashed out via the YouTube video site against her husband Philip Smith, the most powerful theatre-operator on Broadway.

In a tearful and angry video that has attracted thousands of viewings, Walsh-Smith complains that her husband had filed divorce proceedings for no reason, and was evicting her from their luxury apartment by invoking a clause in their pre-nuptial agreement. Furthermore, she reveals highly intimate details of their private life, bringing, in the words of one New York divorce lawyer, 'the concept of humiliation to a whole new level'.

The use of a video-sharing website to fire a salvo in a divorce battle, as Walsh-Smith has done, might well produce some unlikely evidence in court. Thanks to YouTube, however, it is the court of public opinion that is currently making its vote. The public broadcasting of private lives looks to remain one of the most dominant themes of the decade.